BUREAUCRACY,
POLITICS,
AND
PUBLIC POLICY

Bureaucracy,
Politics,
and
Public Policy

Francis E. Rourke
Johns Hopkins University

LITTLE, BROWN AND COMPANY · BOSTON

LIBRARY OF CONGRESS CATALOG CARD NO. 68–26346

FIFTH PRINTING

PUBLISHED SIMULTANEOUSLY IN CANADA
BY LITTLE, BROWN & COMPANY (CANADA) LIMITED

PRINTED IN THE UNITED STATES OF AMERICA

For Kathy, Steve,
and Anne

Preface

One approach to public bureaucracy which has won increasing favor in recent years is to look upon government agencies as part of the family of organizations — sharing common problems with churches, factories, trade unions, and a host of other private institutions. The emergence of an organization theory with a scope as wide as society itself has had an enormously stimulating effect upon the study of public administration. It has introduced a whole new range of explanatory concepts as a guide to understanding the behavior of public officials.

At the same time, however, an appreciation of the characteristics which public agencies share with private organizations should not be allowed to obscure the unique function of these agencies as instruments of the state intimately involved in the development and execution of public policy. It is the role of bureaucracy in the policy process which is at the center of concern in this book. For it is in the crucible of administrative politics today that public policy is mainly hammered out, through bargaining, negotiation, and conflict among appointed rather than elected officials. The bureaucratization of the policy process is particularly pronounced in defense and foreign affairs, but it reaches into domestic policy as well. The design and operation of the policy systems in which bureaucracies participate has thus become a primary item on the agenda of contemporary political science.

This study is largely based on materials drawn from the American experience. Consequently, it applies more directly to the interaction between bureaucracy and public policy in the United States than it does to other political systems. Certain features of the policy process that are examined, especially the extensive involvement of executive agencies in the task of creating and nursing a constituency, are almost distinctively American. In the so-called emerging nations, for example — where political institutions are characteristically quite undeveloped — bureaucratic power tends to rest on a monopoly of expertise and command of the formal apparatus of the state. However, the American pattern has many parallels elsewhere, and, as the most advanced industrial system in the world, it may well represent a model toward which other societies will eventually evolve.

Needless to say, I have incurred a great many debts in the course of preparing this manuscript. This debt is obvious in the case of the authors cited in the footnotes and bibliography. Without their assistance, the book could not have been written.

Less obvious is the contribution of those whose assistance has been more personal. Without involving them in any way in mistakes or failures on my part, I would like to express my gratitude to Professors Alan Altshuler, Jerome Gilison and Robert W. Tucker for reading the manuscript and making many suggestions toward its improvement.

In working on this study, I had the assistance of three very able graduate assistants, Virginia Ermer, Aubrey King and Paul Lutzker. Mrs. Ermer helped proofread the manuscript, Mr. King did much of the work involved in preparing the bibliography which appears at the end of the book, and Mr. Lutzker's resourcefulness was a constant asset to me.

All the graduate students in my seminar in public administration read the manuscript and gave me the benefit of their sagacious and irreverent comments.

With her customary and still somewhat incredible efficiency, Mrs. Catherine Grover typed the manuscript, correcting my errors as she went along.

Finally, at Little Brown, I would like to record my appreciation to Mr. Donald R. Hammonds, who started me on this project, and Mr. David L. Giele, who helped bring it to completion.

Francis E. Rourke
Johns Hopkins University

Contents

BUREAUCRACY,
POLITICS,
AND
PUBLIC POLICY

CHAPTER ONE

Introduction:
The Bureaucratic
Policy System

The belief that power in the modern state has come increasingly to be centered in the corridors of bureaucracy is more often asserted or assumed than examined. This book is an inquiry into the nature of the role which bureaucrats play in making policy decisions in contemporary government. It focuses both on the roots of bureaucratic power — the source from which administrative agencies derive their influence on the policy process — and on the distinctive problems that arise when policy-making is carried on within a bureaucratic setting.

The power of government agencies can be looked upon as resting essentially on political support. Agencies have power when they command the allegiance of fervent and substantial constituencies. From this perspective, the study of administrative policy-making can be readily assimilated into the traditional group analysis of American political life. Agencies provide channels of "access" through which segments of the public can advance or protect their interests in the executive branch in much the same way as they pursue their goals through other governmental institutions — the political parties, the legislature and even the judiciary.[1]

Certainly, there is no disputing the fact that a great deal of administrative influence can be explained within the framework of

[1] See, in this regard, the analysis of administrative activity as part of the group system of politics in David B. Truman, *The Governmental Process* (New York: Alfred A. Knopf, 1951), pp. 395–478 and Harmon Zeigler, *Interest Groups in American Society* (Englewood Cliffs, N.J.: Prentice-Hall, 1964), pp. 277–299.

group theory. As the following chapter will show, it is the agitation of outside groups which commonly leads to the establishment of executive agencies, and agencies and groups are bound together on a day-to-day basis through a wide variety of mutually rewarding relationships. This is especially true in the case of executive agencies administering domestic programs in an area such as natural resources, where it is often true to say that administrative influence rests entirely on public support, or, as one author puts it, "power is organized around constituency."[2]

It would, however, be short-sighted to regard all administrative power as the exclusive product of an agency's success in mobilizing interest group support. While bureaucracy is part of the system through which the values and aspirations of various segments of the community are incorporated into public policy, it is more than a mere conduit through which these outside groups can exercise influence upon government decisions. Within its own ranks, public bureaucracy numbers a wide variety of highly organized and technically trained professional personnel, whose knowledge and skills powerfully influence the shape of official decision. While bureaucratic policy-making in many fields has been primarily a reflection of the system of group pressures, there are other areas such as science and national defense where the expertise and informational resources of bureaucratic organizations have themselves been controlling factors in the development of public policy.

In most cases policy decisions within bureaucracy represent the outcome of a process of interaction between these two sources of power — the needs or aspirations of groups within the community with which executive agencies are allied and the expertise of bureaucrats themselves. However, as far as constituency pressures are concerned, it should be noted that executive agencies can articulate as well as echo the interests of important segments of the community. One of the increasingly important functions of bureaucracy in contemporary society is to provide a means of effective expression in policy deliberations for community groups that are inarticulate, poorly organized, or for some other reason unable to speak for themselves. These step-children of the political system may acquire with administrative help a political equality with other

[2] Matthew Holden, Jr., "'Imperialism' in Bureaucracy," *American Political Science Review*, Vol. LX (Dec., 1966), p. 951.

groups they could never hope to attain through the ordinary processes of politics alone.

Bureaucrats thus generate as well as mirror the group pressures which play so important a role in the development of public policy today. Moreover, there are many issues, especially in foreign policy, where "decisions are made by high public and private 'officials' in virtually a public opinion and interest-group opinion vacuum." [3] In areas of this sort, bureaucrats are in a commanding position to influence the shape of public policy since they possess not only the professional skills necessary to devise rational courses of action but also the ability to structure the public attitudes and preferences to which their policy decisions are in theory supposed to respond. In such situations executive agencies may come close to exercising monopoly power over the development of public policy.

RESPONSIVENESS AND EFFECTIVENESS

The way in which policy decisions are made within bureaucracy — or what might be called the bureaucratic policy system — has traditionally been designed in terms of two criteria. The first is the responsiveness of the system — the extent to which it promotes a correspondence between the decisions of bureaucrats and the preferences of the community or the office-holders who presume to speak for the public. The second is the effectiveness of the system — the degree to which it leads to decisions which are more likely than alternative choices to bring about the outcomes that are desired. Responsiveness and effectiveness are thus the touchstones by which we commonly measure the utility of a bureaucratic policy system.

At all levels of government in the United States, the task of creating an acceptable policy system has been enormously complicated by the fact that the criteria of responsiveness and effectiveness often point in opposite directions. Organizational arrangements and procedures that appear perfectly designed to enhance the responsiveness of the bureaucratic policy system frequently seem least likely to produce effective decisions.

In national security administration, for example, the effectiveness

---

[3] Theodore J. Lowi, "American Business, Public Policy, Case Studies, and Political Theory," *World Politics,* Vol. XVI (July, 1964), p. 680.

of policy-making has usually seemed to demand a high degree of secrecy in bureaucratic deliberations. Apart from the obvious need to prevent disclosure of military or diplomatic information that might be helpful to a foreign adversary, the resort to secrecy in this area of policy has been justified on the grounds that it promotes candor in internal deliberations, and enables the government to gain the advantage of "surprise" in dealing with other states. The success of American policy in the Cuban missile crisis in 1962 has often been traced to the secrecy which surrounded the discussion within the government preceding the final decision to establish a blockade around Cuba.[4]

At the same time, however, the Cuban missile case highlights the fact that arrangements designed to enhance effectiveness in policy-making may clearly preclude the processes of popular consultation which are indispensable if responsiveness is to be secured. Certainly the kind of internal dialogue within bureaucracy that accompanied the Cuban crisis in 1962 could not have taken place in public while officials were considering alternative ways of dealing with the threat to American security that the Soviet missile bases then under construction appeared to represent.

There have been situations, of course, in which effectiveness and responsiveness in bureaucratic policy-making did not seem as incompatible as they did at the time of the confrontation with the Soviets in 1962. For example, after the invasion of Cuba by a refugee group supported by the United States had failed at the Bay of Pigs in 1961, President Kennedy conceded that the mistake of launching this attack might well have been avoided if there had been full disclosure of the plan to the American public and a broader discussion of it.

Thus, in the case of the Bay of Pigs invasion it is possible that both the effectiveness and responsiveness of policy would have been better served by administrative arrangements designed to promote public, rather than secret, decisions. The same argument could be

---

[4] See the discussion of the Cuban missile episode in Arthur M. Schlesinger, Jr., *A Thousand Days* (Boston: Houghton Mifflin, 1965), chaps. 30, 31, and Theodore Sorensen, *Kennedy* (New York: Harper and Row, 1965), pp. 667–718. What is perhaps most remarkable about each of these accounts is the ease with which the authors accept the fact that decisions jeopardizing perhaps the survival of life on this planet should be made by a handful of men acting in secrecy.

made with respect to the U-2 spy flight over the Soviet Union in 1960 and the continuing subsidies to youth organizations and other educational groups by the Central Intelligence Agency until 1967. Even in governmental circles it was widely agreed that these ill-fated ventures in policy might not have been made had it not been for the secrecy which surrounded official decision.

Cases of this kind have led some observers to conclude that — from the point of view of effectiveness alone — the bureaucratic policy system should be as "open" as possible. Secrecy, it is argued, allows officials to cover up and continue ill-advised policies and to shield their own incompetence from discovery. A system of disclosure, on the other hand, has a variety of practical advantages. For one thing it enables the President and other responsible executives to obtain better information on what is going on within the agencies they are supposed to supervise. Moreover, by widening the circle of those allowed to participate in policy discussions, an open system enables policy decisions to be informed by the advice and suggestions of many knowledgeable individuals who would otherwise be excluded from the deliberative process altogether.

Certainly, it is clear that there are a good many situations in which disclosure contributes to the effectiveness as well as the responsiveness of the policy-making process. It would greatly simplify the task of designing a bureaucratic policy system if this were the universal situation. Unfortunately, no such convenient correspondence between the requirements of responsiveness and the need for effectiveness can always be anticipated. While administrative arrangements designed to secure full publicity for all aspects of bureaucratic policy deliberations would help to prevent some mistakes in policy, they would also guarantee fewer successes. Not only in foreign affairs, such as the Cuban missile case previously cited, but also in domestic policy-making there are many situations in which the ability of executive agencies to carry on discussions in private while alternative policies are being considered is essential to the effectiveness of the decision.

Consequently, in the design of policy systems, it is not always possible to escape the difficult problem of devising arrangements which will help achieve quite contradictory goals. Gains in the effectiveness of the policy process may have to be paid for by some losses in its responsiveness, and it cannot always be assumed that measures designed to enhance responsiveness will not jeopardize the effectiveness of the system.

The need to reconcile such conflicting claims often produces innovation in the design of the policy system. If traditional methods of insuring the responsiveness of an executive agency seem incompatible with its effectiveness, then new methods may have to be devised. When, for example, the Central Intelligence Agency was established in 1947 it was clear to all concerned that the operations of an agency of this kind required secrecy for their effectiveness and that the agency could not, therefore, be subject to the same kind of public surveillance as other administrative organizations. Arrangements were devised for subjecting the CIA to a system of controls by other governmental units, such as a presidential advisory committee, which also operates largely in secret.[5]

DESIGNING A POLICY SYSTEM

Even when there has been agreement on the need to maintain both effectiveness and responsiveness in the design of the bureaucratic policy system, there has not always been a meeting of minds on what each of these criteria requires. For some observers, responsiveness may simply entail the right of the public to determine what the ultimate objectives of bureaucratic activity shall be. By others it may be extended to include control by the public or its representatives of the day-to-day actions and decisions in which executive agencies engage in order to achieve these fundamental goals. It has long been argued whether legislatures should be confined to spelling out statutory guidelines for agency action, or encouraged in addition to monitor, as they often do, the processes and procedures through which agencies pursue their statutory purposes.

Similar problems arise with respect to the distribution of authority in the bureaucratic policy system. In national administration, and increasingly at lower levels of government as well, responsiveness has been widely believed to require the centralization of authority in the hands of top executives. The assumption is

[5] For a well-balanced discussion of the controls now exercised over the CIA, see Harry Howe Ransom, *Can American Democracy Survive Cold War?* (Garden City, N.Y.: Doubleday Anchor Books, 1964), pp. 165–195. As Ransom indicates, these controls still leave the CIA substantially free of the outside scrutiny to which other agencies are subject.

made that when authority is centered at the commanding heights of bureaucracy, the public can more easily identify the officials responsible for decision and influence their conduct. However, in the practice of some units of government as well as in the literature of public administration, it is still possible to find support for the position that responsiveness requires a bureaucratic system in which authority is widely dispersed. Such dispersion, it is held, enables bureaucrats to develop more intimate ties with the groups in the community immediately affected by the programs they are carrying out, and makes them more sensitive to the aspirations of these constituencies.

Effectiveness can also be an ambiguous goal. In the period prior to World War II, concern over the effectiveness of the bureaucratic policy system largely centered on the need to increase the ability of executives to control and direct the organizational units under their jurisdiction. Implicit in this approach was the assumption that the capacity of executive agencies to choose intelligent courses of action could be taken for granted. The problems of management were identified as essentially those of mobilizing the energy and resources of executive agencies toward the achievement of these agreed-upon goals. A notable example of this orientation toward the task of insuring effectiveness in public administration was the report issued in 1937 by the President's Committee on Administrative Management.

Increasingly in recent years, however, concern with the effectiveness in the bureaucratic policy system has come to center on the development of techniques for arriving at better decisions. Since it is now generally recognized that bureaucrats make, as well as carry out, policies, the quality of their decisions becomes as important as the manner of their execution. Illustrations of this new approach to effectiveness in public administration include the growing reliance on cost-benefit analysis in choosing between alternative uses for public funds. This technique is labeled the "cost-effectiveness" ratio in national defense policy.

Thus, the institutional arrangements through which the goals of responsiveness and effectiveness are sought in the bureaucratic policy system are changeable. But the desire to achieve these goals has been a constant objective from the first emergence of bureaucracy as an independent factor of major importance in American government in the late nineteenth and early twentieth centuries.

SCOPE OF THIS STUDY

Part One of this analysis focuses on the factors which account for the great influence bureaucrats now exert on policy decisions. Chapter Two deals with the political sources of this impact — the ability of executive agencies to build support by mobilizing a constituency. In Chapter Three, attention is shifted to bureaucratic expertise as a means of controlling the policy process. Executive agencies are rich repositories of specialized skills, and they can as a result mold policy decisions in many areas in which outside pressures hardly exist. Chapter Four concludes this analysis of bureaucratic power with an examination of the reasons why some agencies have much more influence on policy decisions than others.

In Part Two, the policy process itself is the central concern. Chapter Five examines the character of bureaucratic policy-making. Who are the principal participants in the decision-making process within executive agencies, and what impact does the bureaucratic environment itself have upon policy outcomes? Chapter Six presents an appraisal of current efforts to re-design the system through which bureaucratic policy is shaped. Increasingly, attempts are being made to broaden the perspectives of policy-makers, to increase the reliability of the data on which decisions are based, and to enhance the capacity of executive agencies for more original and creative thought.

Finally, in Chapter Seven, we return to the question which has been implicit throughout this discussion. Does the mounting influence of bureaucracy over all phases of policy in the modern state mean that a new power elite has emerged — controlling all decisions but itself uncontrolled? This is a key problem not only in American politics but in every political system today. Certainly it is of compelling importance in the politics of the newly emerging nations. Here bureaucratic power, particularly in the form of military organizations, is highly developed, while the governmental institutions through which this power can be contained, such as political parties and the judiciary, remain at a primitive stage of evolution.

Part One

THE SOURCES OF POWER

CHAPTER TWO

The Mobilization
of Political
Support

A first and fundamental source of power for administrative agencies in American society is their ability to attract outside support. Strength in a constituency is no less an asset for an American administrator than it is for a politician, and some agencies have succeeded in building outside support as formidable as that of any political organization. The lack of such support severely circumscribes the ability of an agency to achieve its goals, and may even threaten its survival as an organization. As Norton Long puts it: "The bureaucracy under the American political system has a large share of responsibility for the public promotion of policy and even more in organizing the political basis for its survival and growth." [1]

This entanglement with politics has been a characteristic of American administration since at least the days of President Andrew Jackson. The intrusions of politics came first from the political parties, anxious to use administrative jobs as building blocks in the construction of party organizations. However, beginning with the Pendleton Act in 1883, the ability of political parties to exploit administrative agencies in this way was increasingly subject to legal restriction. Slowly but surely, the principle came to be accepted that appointments to career positions in the public service

[1] Norton Long, *The Polity* (Chicago: Rand McNally & Co., 1962), p. 53.

should go to those who are technically qualified without regard to their party affiliation.[2]

But this development by no means banished politics from American administration. Since American political parties did not function effectively as organizations for the development and support of policy objectives, administrative agencies were forced to develop their own basis of political support, negotiating alliances in and out of government with a variety of groups that could be used to advance bureaucratic objectives or to assist an agency in fending off attack. The political neutralization of bureaucracy is impossible in a country in which the political parties are incapable of performing the functions expected of them in the governmental structure of which they are a part. When the parties do not provide for program development and the mobilization of political support, executive agencies must perform these tasks for themselves.

From the point of view of an administrative agency, there are three vital centers from which political support may be drawn: the outside community, the legislature, and the executive branch itself. All these sources of political strength may be cultivated simultaneously, and usually are; or one may be nursed virtually to the exclusion of the others. The possibility of choice often calls for the exercise of administrative statecraft of a high order to balance one source of strength against another, in this way building an enclave of political independence. Sometimes, however, no choice is possible. A state treasurer directly elected by the legislature cannot easily look elsewhere for political support. An executive budget office is, in most circumstances, politically captive to the chief executive it serves. If he does not choose to give it political standing, then it has none. These and other possibilities will be examined in the pages that follow, as each of the various ways in which administrative agencies build political support is examined in turn.

BUREAUCRACY AND ITS PUBLICS

Basic to any agency's political standing in the American system of government is the support of public opinion. If it has that, an

2 For a careful analysis of this development over the course of American history, see Herbert Kaufman, "The Growth of the Federal Personnel System," in Wallace Sayre (editor), *The Federal Government Service* (Englewood Cliffs, N.J.: Prentice-Hall, 1965), pp. 7–69.

agency can ordinarily expect to be strong in the legislative and the executive branch as well. Since public opinion is ultimately the only legitimate sovereign in a democratic society, an agency which seeks first a high standing with the public can reasonably expect to have all other things added unto it in the way of legislative and executive support. Power gives power, in administration as elsewhere, and once an agency has established a secure base with the public, it cannot easily be trifled with by political officials in either the legislative or executive branch.

There are essentially two ways in which public support may be cultivated. The first is by creating a favorable attitude toward the agency in the public at large. The second is by building strength with "attentive" publics — groups which have a salient interest in the agency — usually because it has the capacity to provide them with some significant benefit, or the power to exercise regulatory authority in ways that may be of critical importance to the groups concerned.

Again these methods are not mutually exclusive. An agency can certainly seek to create general public support while assiduously building alliances with interest groups which have a special stake in its work. This is in fact the strategy most agencies follow, to the extent that is available to them. Actually, only a comparatively few agencies carry on functions that have a high degree of visibility for the general public. An agency like the FBI, which has been performing a dramatic role in American life for several decades, does command a broad pattern of public support that stretches throughout all strata of society. Part of this public standing may be said to spring from skillful use of publicity by agencies like the FBI — an ability to exploit every opportunity to catch the public eye with the achievements of the agency. But the power of publicity, even in America, is not boundless, and an agency whose activities do not match the FBI's in intrinsic dramatic appeal will not equal it in public esteem no matter how assiduously it carries on public relations activity.[3]

There may be occasions, of course, when any agency may find itself

---

[3] For analysis of the power of government publicity, see Douglass Cater, *The Fourth Branch of Government* (Boston: Houghton Mifflin Co., 1959); J. A. R. Pimlott, *Public Relations and American Democracy* (Princeton: Princeton University Press, 1951); and Francis E. Rourke, *Secrecy and Publicity: Dilemmas of Democracy* (Baltimore: The Johns Hopkins Press, 1961).

basking temporarily in the limelight of publicity. The Food and
Drug Administration, for example, may languish out of sight as far
as the general public is concerned, until suddenly the injurious effects of a new drug arouses public concern, as was the case a few
years ago with thalidomide, a tranquilizer whose use by pregnant
women brought about the delivery of a large number of infants
with birth deformities. Immediately, the agency and its pronounce-
ments became a matter of front-page interest. For a brief period at
least, it was an organization with a very extensive public indeed.
Or, a state air pollution commission, conducting its affairs in almost
total obscurity, may suddenly find itself projected to the forefront
of public attention by the onset of severe atmospheric smog, as
occurred along the Eastern seaboard in the fall of 1966. In a case
of this kind, the head of such an agency may find himself an over-
night celebrity.

What these illustrations suggest is the fact that many agencies
have a potential public that far exceeds the size of their normal
constituency. The existence of such a potential public reflects the
fact that an agency carries on activities which affect the interests
of a far larger group than the public which consistently identifies
itself with its program. Both the food and drug and air pollution
agencies are in the public health field, where agencies perform
functions that are of vital importance to a general public which
may not even be aware of their existence. However, if events arouse
the attention of this latent public, the agency's power in the
community and the legislature may suddenly swell in importance.
To the extent that it depends upon a broad pattern of public
support, administrative power may thus be extremely volatile,
shifting — like a politician's — with changing tides of public opinion.

Hence, it is essential to every agency's power position to have the
support of attentive groups whose attachment is grounded on an
enduring tie of tangible interest. The groups an agency directly
serves provide the most natural basis of such political support, and
it is with these interest groups that agencies ordinarily establish the
firmest alliances. Such groups have often been responsible for the
establishment of the agency in the first place. Thereafter, the agency
and the group are bound together by deeply rooted ties that may
be economic, political, or social in character. From an economic per-

spective, the agency usually carries on activities that advance the material welfare of members of the group. The group in turn may supply private employment opportunities for employees of the agency. Also, in return for the political representation with which the agency provides the group in the executive apparatus, the group ordinarily supports the agency in a variety of undertakings, including its requests for financial support, its attempts to secure the passage of legislation expanding its powers, or its efforts to defend itself against legislative proposals which threaten its administrative status. Finally, frequent social contact between agency and group breeds ties of familiarity and friendship that help seal the alliance. In its most developed form, the relationship between an interest group and an administrative agency is so close that it is difficult to know where the group leaves off and the agency begins.

This identity between an interest group and an executive agency is strongly reinforced by the practice, especially common at the state level, of having occupational requirements as a qualification for appointment to administrative office. Under law, the members of a state real estate commission may have to be licensed real estate brokers, and similar requirements often prevail with respect to other administrative boards having the power of occupational licensing in the states. This arrangement merely gives formal legal blessing to the common political practice of allowing interest groups to have a major voice in, if not a veto power over, appointments to agencies which administer functions in which they have a vital stake. Legal support for interest group involvement in the affairs of administrative agencies may also come from statutes requiring group representation on agency advisory committees, or the legal stipulation, common, for example, in agricultural administration, that the agency secure the consent of interest group members before exercising certain regulatory powers. There are also cases — the administration of grazing on public lands in the West, for example — where individuals representative of interest groups are given the power to enforce administrative regulations at the point of impact.[4]

Agencies that are not in a position to dispense important bene-

4 See Phillip O. Foss, *Politics and Grass* (Seattle: University of Washington Press, 1960).

fits or favors to any segment of the community are in a disadvantageous position with respect to their ability to attract organized group
support. The State Department is commonly regarded as having
no "natural constituency" in the sense of groups for which the department is able to do tangible and significant favors. Even though
the fate of the entire population may depend on the effective conduct of foreign affairs, there is no strongly organized group structure in the outside community which regards the department as
"its department," and stands ready to defend and assist it in attaining its goals.

However, even the State Department has been able to identify
more than 300 groups with which it maintains close liaison on
foreign policy matters.[5] And some of these groups can exercise
substantial influence over the conduct of foreign affairs. In 1964,
for example, the International Longshoreman's Association refused
to load wheat on ships destined for the Soviet Union and other
Communist countries. This refusal seriously embarrassed the department in the efforts it was then making to improve relations
with the Eastern European countries.

For many of these outside organizations, however, the work of
the department is of secondary rather than primary importance.
Their interest in foreign affairs is something less than an intense
preoccupation. Hence, in order to secure public backing on matters
of major concern to it, the department has often had to resort to
organizing outside group support itself. If the mountain will not
come to Mahomet, Mahomet will go to the mountain. The organization by the department of a blue-ribbon committee of distinguished citizens to lead a campaign in behalf of the Marshall Plan
in 1947 is an illustration of the department's success in establishing
its own public support,[6] and this kind of stratagem has been used
by the department to accomplish a variety of other foreign policy
objectives. In 1967, for example, a committee of distinguished citizens was organized to support President Johnson's Vietnam policies
and was given the ringing title of Citizens Committee for Peace
with Freedom in Vietnam.

[5] See W. O. Chittick, *The Domestic Information Activities of the Department of State* (unpublished Ph.D. dissertation, The Johns Hopkins University,
1964), p. 158.
[6] See Richard E. Neustadt, *Presidential Power* (New York: John Wiley &
Sons, 1960), pp. 49–50.

Executive agencies like the State Department can in fact be extremely adroit in organizing pressures upon themselves to which they seem to be responding, but which they are in fact initiating. The organization of such apparent pressure group activity thus provides a means by which these agencies can conceal their own central role in the policy process. The initiative appears to be with outside organizations, but the activities of these external groups are actually instigated by the agency itself. However, one risk an agency runs in this connection is that the mass opinion it is helping to create may eventually be a constraint upon it when and if it decides to change the policies for which it is currently seeking public support.

The State Department is by no means the only administrative agency to organize its own infra-structure of interest group support. The Department of Agriculture played a principal role in the organization and development of the American Farm Bureau Federation — the largest and most powerful of the agricultural interest group organizations.[7] And very early in its history the Department of Labor became convinced that the only way in which it could reach the wage-earning clientele it was obligated to serve was by encouraging the development of trade unions. Labor organizations provided an avenue for the dissemination of the informational material that was, in the beginning, the department's chief contribution to improvement of the welfare of its wage-earner clientele. The department had to communicate with its constituency, and, as it was to point out itself: "Freely as conferences with unorganized wage earners are welcome, official intercourse with individuals as such has practical limits which organization alone can remove."

Not only did the department thus defend its close liaison with existing trade union organizations; it also came, not illogically in view of the need to facilitate communication with its clientele, to support the extension of trade union organization among wage earners. The reason the department gave for this support was that the growth of labor union membership would facilitate collective bargaining and promote industrial peace. "The absence of organization," the department stated, "means the absence of a medium

7 See David B. Truman, *The Governmental Process* (New York: Alfred A. Knopf, 1951), pp. 90–92.

through which the workers *en masse* can discuss their problems with employers. The denial of this organization is the denial of the only means of peaceable settlement they have." Such pragmatic considerations were involved in the department's support of expanded trade unionism as the fact that the strengthening of wage-earner organizations would increase the size of the department's effective clientele and the weight of its political support.[8]

Perhaps the worst hazard an agency faces, when it deliberately sets out to establish an infra-structure of interest group support, is the possibility that, once established, these groups may break away from agency control, or even become a focus of opposition to it. The parent-teacher associations set up in conjunction with school systems at the local level generally play a useful role in providing citizen support for education officials. But if these PTA organizations are captured by opponents of the existing educational system, as has occurred in some areas, then they provide a formidable vehicle for mobilizing opposition to school administrators — more effective, because of their semi-official status, than any other organizational resource at the disposal of critics of the educational establishment.

One of the major advantages the support of interest groups has for an executive department is the fact that such groups can often do for a department things that it cannot very easily do for itself. Interest groups can take a position on policy questions that department officials secretly hold but cannot publicly advocate because it may put them in disfavor with the President. The outside groups which support each of the various branches of the armed forces in the Department of Defense have often given military officials assistance in precisely this way. As Huntington puts it:

> The allies and supporters of a service are at times more royalist than the king. They do not necessarily identify more intensely with service interests than do the members of the service, but they do have a greater freedom to articulate those interests and to promote them through a wider variety of political means.[9]

[8] Francis E. Rourke, "The Department of Labor and the Trade Unions," *The Western Political Quarterly*, Vol. VII (December, 1954), pp. 661–662.

[9] Samuel P. Huntington, *The Common Defense: Strategic Programs in National Politics* (New York: Columbia University Press, 1961), p. 397.

While deference to their commander-in-chief may not permit military officials to disagree with the President when he cuts their appropriation or gives another service jurisdiction over a weapons system they believe to be rightfully theirs, no such restrictions prevent defense industries with which they have contractual relations from springing to their defense, or keep a back-stop association, such as the Navy League and the Air Force Association, from vociferous protest against these efforts to trim the appropriations or the jurisdiction of a military agency.

Outside organizations thus play a valuable role in enabling administrative agencies to oppose directives from the chief executive. They are also useful in helping these agencies evade legislative controls. Congress has enacted statutes designed to prevent administrative agencies from propagandizing the public in their own behalf, or lobbying in the legislature to secure the passage of bills they favor. But agencies can escape these restrictions by having outside organizations carry on such public relations or lobbying activity for them. Senator Goldwater once observed that "the aircraft industry has probably done more to promote the Air Force than the Air Force has done itself." [10] This kind of claim could be made for a great variety of interest groups that identify and associate themselves with the fortunes of an executive agency.

The help received from interest groups is not without its perils for an administrative agency. The agency may come to lean so heavily on the political support of an outside group that the group in time acquires a veto power over many of the agency's major decisions. In extreme cases of this kind, the agency becomes in effect a "captive" organization — unable to move in any direction except those permitted it by the group upon which it is politically dependent.

Administrative units that are assumed to be particularly subject to domination of this sort are clientele agencies — public organizations established to provide comprehensive services to a special segment of the population. On the national scene such clientele agencies include the Veterans Administration, the Department of Agriculture, the Children's Bureau, and the Department of Labor. Each of these agencies has a long history of close association with

[10] *Ibid.*, p. 400.

and subordination to outside organizations representative of its clientele.

As noted earlier, the Department of Labor has from its very beginning been closely identified with the trade union movement. When it was first set up in 1913, the department was, as Samuel Gompers put it, intended to be "Labor's Voice in the Cabinet." While this relationship has been helpful in many ways, it has also tended to narrow the scope of the department's authority. For one thing, the trade unions have long been allowed to exercise a great deal of influence over major departmental decisions — including the selection of Assistant Secretaries of Labor. In addition, this association with the union movement made the department suspect in the eyes of other groups — employers, for example — and for a long time its jurisdiction over labor activities has been limited by the reluctance of business and agricultural groups to allow the department to administer functions where its bias in favor of the trade unions might be disadvantageous to their interests. As this illustration makes clear, an agency makes enemies as well as friends when it identifies itself with a particular population group, since it inherits hostilities directed at the group with which it has entered into an alliance.

The submissive posture of a clientele agency toward its constituency is not, of course, a permanent genuflection. During the Eisenhower administration, for example, the Assistant Secretaries of Labor were not chosen by the trade unions. As compared with other periods in its history, the Veterans Administration displayed a great deal of independence from the veterans groups with which it is allied when it was headed by General Omar Bradley — a career officer with a distinguished record in World War II. Leadership by a vigorous personality may thus uncover latitude for independent action by a clientele agency that previously had not been thought possible.

The tendency of clientele agencies to fall under the control of the groups they serve has often been used as an argument against organizing the executive branch upon the basis of the clientele principle.[11] The contention is made that executive agencies can

[11] In his classic statement of traditional organization theory, Gulick, for example, warns against the tendency of the clientele principle to engender "dominance by favor-seeking pressure groups." See Luther Gulick and L. Urwick (eds.), *Papers on the Science of Administration* (New York: Institute of Public Administration, 1937), p. 26.

be prevented from becoming the tools of political groups only if administrative tasks are divided on the basis of some other principle of organizational design. But, in point of fact, it is difficult to identify a principle of organization which will not engender a very close relationship between an administrative agency and the groups which benefit from the activities it carries on. In terms of classical organization theory, the principal alternatives to clientele as a basis for allocating tasks among administrative agencies are the criteria of function to be performed, process or skill to be carried on by agency personnel, or geographical area to be served. However, agencies organized on the basis of function, such as highway, welfare, or education departments, are also susceptible to domination by outside groups, as are agencies organized on the process or skill criterion — the Corps of Engineers, for example.

As far as organization in terms of area is concerned, Selznick's classic study of the interaction between a public agency and its environment — *TVA and the Grass Roots* [12] — clearly revealed a pervasive pattern of outside control ·over the foremost agency of the national government organized on the basis of geographical area, the Tennessee Valley Authority. In return for the support it received from important groups in the Valley area, the TVA proceeded to modify many of the original objectives of its agricultural program that were offensive to this constituency.

Of course in its own defense, the agency could point out that the goals it modified were not of salient importance to it, that its real concern was with its public power program in the Tennessee Valley, and if support for this activity could only be obtained by "selling out," so to speak, on agricultural goals, then this was an exchange well worth making. Selznick himself later conceded the validity of such a strategy:

> . . . the TVA purchased a considerable advantage with these concessions. It gained the support of important local interests and of a powerful national lobby. These defended not only the agricultural program but TVA as a whole. In this way, by modifying its agricultural program and certain broad social policies, the Authority was able to ward off threatened dismemberment and to gain time for the successful develop-

[12] Philip Selznick, *TVA and the Grass Roots* (Berkeley: University of California Press, 1949).

ment of its key activity — the expansion of electric power
facilities.[13]

Any public agency may thus find it necessary to yield control
over a segment of its program to a significant interest group in
order to buy the support of that group for more important policy
goals. A state university, for example, may tailor its program of
agricultural education to fit the needs of important farm groups,
so as to obtain the support, or at least neutralize the opposition of
rural groups to certain educational activities in science and the
humanities. Some of an agency's activities may thus serve as "loss
leaders" — activities that represent a loss or at least small profit from
the point of view of an agency's major goals, but that simultaneously widen the basis of political support for objectives that are of
more significance to it. In the case of a state university again, its
intercollegiate football program may represent just such a "loss
leader." The support engendered by the achievements of its football team may quicken the allegiance of alumni and other citizen
groups to the university in areas of science and culture far removed
from the gridiron.

There is always the possibility that this kind of support will be
purchased at the price of serious damage to major institutional
goals. Activities that are initially designed to be merely supportive
in character may in time grow so large as to have wide-ranging and
debilitating effects upon an institution's capacity to achieve its
major goals. In the case of the state university, for example, its
agricultural school may dominate the image a university radiates
to the outside world, and this reputation as a "cow college" may
seriously handicap its ability to attract faculty and students for
non-agricultural programs. Or a football program established to
win support for academic activities may eventually lead to a serious
dilution in educational quality as standards are lowered in order
to recruit athletic talent.

Goal distortion of a serious kind is thus always a possible price
of constituency support. The worst illustrations of this have occurred in the area of regulatory administration. At both the state
and national level of government, agencies established to regulate

[13] Philip Selznick, *Leadership in Administration* (Evanston, Illinois: Row,
Peterson & Co., 1957), p. 44.

particular kinds of economic activity have always exhibited an extraordinary penchant for falling under the control of the groups
placed under their jurisdiction. The regulatory agency thus becomes in effect the pawn of the regulated industry. This kind of
relationship represents a radical inversion of organizational goals,
as an agency enters into collusion with the very group whose behavior it is supposed to control.[14]

While it is easy to censure this kind of collusion, a close relationship between a regulatory agency and the groups under its jurisdiction is often essential to an agency's achievement of its goals. In the
case of an air pollution commission, for example, the effectiveness
of the commission may be enormously enhanced by including
in its membership representatives of some of the principal industries responsible for the discharge of waste materials into the
atmosphere. These representatives can help secure the compliance
of their firms with air pollution regulations — a consideration which
is especially important when an agency has very little coercive authority and must rely largely on voluntary compliance to achieve
its regulatory goals. In its inception, at least, cooperation with the
groups it is trying to control may thus be functional for a regulatory agency. It becomes dysfunctional only when, at some further
point in the relationship, an agency modifies or even abandons its
goals in order to retain group support.

Generally speaking, in the case of clientele, regulatory, and other
administrative agencies, the tendency for capture by an outside
group to take place is greatest when an agency deals with a single-
interest constituency. In a case of this kind, an agency has nowhere
else to turn if the group upon which it depends should threaten to
withdraw its support. Diversification of support is as desirable for
a government agency as product diversification is for a private business firm. Consider the case of grazing administration:

> The Grazing Service suffered because of its rather complete
> dependence on stockmen and those who spoke for them in
> Congress. By merging the Service into an expanded Bureau of

14 For an analysis of this tendency in regulatory agencies, see Marver H.
Bernstein, *Regulating Business by Independent Commission* (Princeton, N.J.:
Princeton University Press, 1955), pp. 74–102. Bernstein argues that all regulatory agencies go through a "life cycle" in which capture by the regulated groups
is a culminating phase.

Land Management, an act accomplished with the aid of interests adversely affected under the previous arrangement, the
new organization has reduced its dependence by being able to
appeal to a broader constituency.[15]

The heterogeneity of an administrative agency's group support thus
seems to be more important in determining its freedom of action
than the question of whether it is organized on the basis of clientele, purpose, process, or area to be served. The design of its political
system, rather than its organizational structure, is the critical consideration.

For all agencies it is highly important to keep abreast of changes
in the structure of interests affected by the activities they carry on.
Huntington traces the administrative decline of the Interstate Commerce Commission to the failure of the agency to develop support
among the new groups that emerged in the twentieth century as
major transportation interests — the truckers, the water carriers, and
the airlines. Instead, the agency tied itself to the railroads — a declining industry it had been originally created to curb in the nineteenth century. "The ICC," Huntington says, "has not responded
to the demands of the new forces in transportation. . . . Consequently, it is losing its leadership to those agencies which are more
responsive to the needs and demands of the times." [16] The establishment in 1966 of the Department of Transportation as the major
transportation agency of the national government provides striking
confirmation of this argument.

LEGISLATIVE SUPPORT

The legislature is a source of political strength for administrative
agencies in essentially two ways. In the first place, it is from laws
enacted by the legislature that agencies derive their basic legal
powers — to give advice, to exercise regulatory authority, or to provide services to the public. Such laws often determine as well the
organizational structure of an agency and its ability to hire person-

[15] Aaron Wildavsky, *The Politics of the Budgetary Process* (Boston: Little,
Brown and Co., 1964), p. 172.
[16] Samuel P. Huntington, "The Marasmus of the I.C.C.: The Commission,
the Railroads, and the Public Interest," *Yale Law Journal*, Vol. 61 (April,
1952), pp. 472–473.

nel, or to engage in a host of other housekeeping activities. Law is a fundamental basis of administrative authority, and it is the legislature which, initially at least, writes the law.

A second reason for administrative dependence upon legislative support is the fact that the money which administrative agencies need to fuel their activities must come through the avenue of appropriation bills passed by the legislature. No matter how broad the scope of an agency's formal authority, its real power turns ultimately upon its fiscal resources. A regulatory agency left without adequate funds to enforce the law which it administers has the shadow but not the substance of power. Similarly, the range of services any agency can provide is determined ultimately by the money it is authorized to spend. Money talks, in administration as elsewhere.

As indicated in the previous section, high standing with the public gives any agency substantial leverage in dealing with the legislature. However, legislative support is not simply a function of public favor. As the work of Fenno on the appropriation process in Congress clearly reveals, an agency can have a great deal of outside support without enjoying a corresponding esteem with influential elites in the legislature. Conversely, there are a number of agencies which are held in very high regard in Congress but leave the public largely indifferent.[17]

Fenno used two yardsticks for measuring agency success in dealing with the House Appropriations Committee and ultimately with Congress itself. The first was the percentage of its request for appropriations which an administrative agency was successful in obtaining from the House Committee. A number of agencies which scored very high in this regard are very little known in the outside community. The Bureau of Customs is one example in this category, and the Bureau of the Public Debt is another. Both of these agencies are in the Treasury Department, which generally enjoys a very high standing in Congress while not having a great deal of visibility with the public generally.

A second index used by Fenno for measuring administrative success in the legislature was the rate of growth over the years 1947 to 1962 in the financial support which an agency received from the

[17] Richard F. Fenno, *The Power of the Purse* (Boston: Little, Brown and Co., 1966).

House Appropriations Committee. Here he discovered that there were several agencies with a very high growth rate which nevertheless were subjected to very deep budget cuts annually by the House Committee, so that their appropriations as a percentage of their requests were not as high as those of other agencies with a lower growth rate. Among the agencies included in this category were the Bureau of Land Management, the Fish and Wildlife Service, and the Bureau of Labor Standards. Conversely, a number of the agencies which had been very successful in avoiding budget cuts showed very little increase in their appropriations over the years.

Success in avoiding cuts from appropriations requests is not, therefore, the same as the ability to obtain a continuously expanding level of support from the House Committee responsible for appropriations. The difference between these two criteria of success is explained by Fenno in these terms: *"High growth rates can be accounted for primarily by factors external to the Committee, whereas the ability to keep budget cuts to a minimum can be accounted for primarily by factors internal to the Committee-agency relationship."* [18] An agency's success in fending off budget cuts in the House is a measure of its good rapport with legislators. Its ability to maintain a continuing increase in its appropriations reflects an expanding demand for its services by significant segments of the public. Alternatively, high standing in the legislature may coincide with strength in the outside community, so that an agency avoids budget cuts while maintaining a high growth rate in its appropriations; or an agency may have the misfortune of being weak in terms of both legislative and public support, in which event it is subject to both budget cuts and a low appropriations growth rate. Illustrations of each of these various possibilities are presented in Table One.

No matter how these data are interpreted, the legislature reveals itself as an independent force of substantial importance in the life of administrative agencies. Good relations with legislators are especially useful when an agency does not enjoy strong support from outside groups, since this rapport provides assurance that an agency's appropriations, while not expanding, will remain reasonably stable. Even agencies with powerful constituencies can help themselves a great deal by cultivating the goodwill of legislators. While congressmen may not be able to prevent the growth of an

18 *Ibid.*, p. 404.

TABLE ONE
AGENCY SUCCESS IN DEALING WITH
CONGRESS AND THE PUBLIC [1]

CONGRESSIONAL SUPPORT

		Strong	*Weak*
PUBLIC SUPPORT	*Strong*	Soil Conservation Service Food and Drug Administration Office of Education Forest Service	Fish and Wildlife Service National Park Service Geological Survey Bureau of Land Management National Bureau of Standards Bureau of Labor Standards
	Weak	Bureau of Customs Bureau of Public Debt	Bureau of Mines Bonneville Power Administration Bureau of Reclamation Census Bureau

SOURCE: The data on which this table is based may be found in Richard F. Fenno, *The Power of the Purse* (Boston: Little, Brown and Co., 1966), pp. 368, 392, 412.

[1] The 6 agencies with strong congressional support received appropriations ranging from 102.1 to 96.9 per cent of their requests from the House Appropriations Committee over the period from 1947 to 1962. The 10 agencies with strong public support achieved an average growth rate in appropriations ranging from 23.0 to 10.7 per cent from 1947 to 1962.

On the other hand, the 10 agencies with weak congressional support received appropriations ranging from 92.9 to 78.1 per cent of their requests from the Appropriations Committee over the period 1947 to 1962. The 6 agencies with weak public support achieved an average growth rate in appropriations ranging from 4.5 to —.5 from 1947 to 1962.

agency's appropriations as the public demand for its services expands, they can substantially retard this rate of growth by cutting back the agency's budget requests each year.

When an agency does have strong external support, it may use this constituency as a device for bringing pressure to bear upon lawmakers to reverse legislative decisions on appropriations that it considers disadvantageous. Not uncommon, for example, is the practice of cutting back on services provided outside groups in the wake of a legislative cut in appropriations. The reduction in services is designed to provoke protests from the agency's clientele to the legislature which will bring about a restoration of at least part of the sum cut from the budget, and this tactic often succeeds.

As a variety of studies of the legislative process make clear, the administrative relationship with the legislature is, in the United

States at least, largely a relationship with legislative committees, or in some cases even subcommittees.[19] The legislators who must be cultivated are the key men who sit on the committees which have significant power over the agency. The chief aim of administrators here is to win these legislators over to a favorable attitude toward the agency and an appreciation of the skill and dedication with which it carries on its work. In more formal terms, the administrator's goal is to socialize committee members, particularly a committee or subcommittee chairman, to the agency's point of view, so that these legislators may become spokesmen for the organization in Congress.

There is, in fact, no better lobbyist for any administrative agency than a legislator. Thus, the most fortunately situated of all agencies are those which can number legislators in some sense as members of their own organization. Each of the Armed Services, for example, has had the good fortune to have a number of legislators included within its reserve units, and while it is difficult to determine how captive a congressman becomes as a result of his reserve status, this relationship certainly ensures an agency of some kind of capital in the form of legislative goodwill. (See Table Two.)

TABLE TWO
LEGISLATORS IN ARMED
FORCES READY RESERVES
(88th Congress — 1963-64)

	House	Senate
Army	29	6
Air Force	19	7
Navy	17	—
Marines	2	1
Coast Guard	1	1
Total [1]	68	15

SOURCE: Congressional Quarterly Weekly Report, Dec. 18, 1964, pp. 2815-2816.

[1] Of these totals 17 congressmen were or had been members of the Armed Services Committees or Defense Appropriations Subcommittees of their branch of Congress.

In addition to the congressmen who were reservists, 204 legislative staff assistants were in reserve units. However, in 1965, Secretary of Defense McNamara issued an order barring congressmen and their assistants from participation in the ready reserves.

[19] Ibid., p. xvi. "No generalizations about Congress are voiced more frequently or held more firmly than those which proclaim the dominance of committee influence in congressional decision-making."

In state administration a highway department may derive a similar advantage from the fact that some state legislators who are attorneys earn fees from title searches conducted for the department, and other state agencies use devices such as the consultantship to bring legislators within their own organizational network.

The relationship between an administrative agency and legislative committees may vary a great deal from one committee to another. In the 1950's the foreign aid agency normally received a much warmer reception from the House Foreign Affairs Committee than it did before either the Government Operations Committee or the subcommittee of the House Appropriations Committee which dealt with foreign aid expenditures. Each of these latter groups was highly critical of the efficiency and effectiveness of the foreign aid program. During the 1960's military officials testifying on the Vietnam war could expect to receive a more favorable treatment from the Senate Armed Services Committee than they could from the Senate Foreign Relations Committee, a large number of whose members were highly critical of American involvement in Southeast Asia. Relations with any single committee may also change with the passage of time, as the agency or the committee alters its personnel, or as public attitudes toward the agency and its program shift.

One of the most consistent differences in the treatment an agency may encounter in Congress is between the committee which considers legislation in the area of its responsibilities and the appropriations subcommittee which decides in effect how much money the agency can spend to achieve its objectives. Usually the legislative committee is program-oriented and is anxious to see that an agency obtains adequate resources with which to achieve its goals, while the appropriations subcommittee is economy-minded and inclined to trim back appropriations that the legislative committee may have authorized. There is great potential for conflict here, and it has flared up on numerous occasions.

An agency may also experience substantial variation in the treatment it receives from the House and the Senate. In his analysis of the appropriations process, Fenno demonstrates that agencies in the Department of the Interior ordinarily do much better in the Senate than they do in the House. He traces this difference to the fact that the western states, in which Department of the Interior

programs are largely carried on, have stronger representation proportionately in the Senate than they do in the House. Moreover, the
Senate Appropriations subcommittee which considers Department
of the Interior budget requests is more heavily weighted with westerners than the corresponding subcommittee in the House.[20]

One official who plays an important role for a growing number
of executive agencies in their efforts to cultivate legislative support
is the congressional liaison officer. The task of this administrative
official is essentially that of keeping in touch with legislators,
answering their requests for information, providing help to their
constituents, or even writing a speech for a congressman. In an
increasingly complex bureaucratic apparatus, liaison officials have
become almost indispensable in enabling legislators to find their
way around the labyrinthine corridors of bureaucracy.

According to data gathered by G. Russell Pipe, these liaison
activities in 1963 "directly involved the full-time services of 500
government employees at a cost of $5,432,938." Pipe found that the
Department of Defense employed nearly half of all liaison employees (230), followed by the Department of State (68) and the Department of Justice (39).[21] It is, however, questionable if liaison officers
can relieve departmental executives of any save the routine chores
of legislative-executive relations. On matters of critical importance
to an agency, such as the passage of legislation affecting the scope
of its power, the task of winning legislative support must inevitably
be assumed by officials at a high level of responsibility.

Moreover, some departmental executives even complain that liaison officials are a burden as well as a help. Spending, as they do, a
great deal of time in congressional offices, liaison personnel may
generate a good many requests for assistance that, as one irate
executive put it, "might never come to us if our liaison man did
not spend a lot of time on Capitol Hill, running into administrative
assistants to congressmen." [22]

The preceding analysis of the efforts of administrative agencies to
secure legislative support has centered on the essential resources

20 *Ibid.*, p. 581.

21 G. Russell Pipe, "Congressional Liaison: The Executive Branch Consolidates Its Relations with Congress," *Public Administration Review*, Vol. XXVI
(Mar., 1966), p. 17.

22 Marver H. Bernstein, *The Job of the Federal Executive* (Washington:
The Brookings Institution, 1958), p. 115.

which the legislature controls and agencies seek to obtain — legal authority and appropriations. It should be noted at this point, however, that in its relations with the legislature, an agency is motivated by a desire not only to obtain these positive assets but also to escape certain punitive sanctions which the legislature has the power to inflict. These sanctions include the exposure of the agency to unpleasant publicity through a highly publicized investigation of its shortcomings, the refusal to approve the appointment of agency executives when a legislative body possesses this power of confirmation, and the veto of certain financial transactions in which the agency may wish to engage. The dependence of administrative agencies upon legislative good-will thus springs from negative as well as positive considerations — the desire to escape penalties as well as to obtain rewards.

POWER IN THE EXECUTIVE BRANCH

Through the assiduous cultivation of legislative and public support, it is possible for an administrative agency to establish a position of virtually complete autonomy within the executive branch. Agencies like the FBI and the Corps of Engineers are — as compared with other administrative units — largely immune from the hierarchical controls exercised by either the President or officials in their own executive department. Historically, therefore, the quest for outside support has often been a divisive force within the organizational structure of American bureaucracy, weakening the identification of departments with the President or of bureaus with their department. Agencies which use outside support to acquire a position of independence within the executive branch may ultimately come to regard themselves as being in some sense congressional rather than presidential agencies.

There are of course administrative units at the other extreme which possess virtually no independent standing with the public or the legislature. Performing functions that are primarily useful within the executive branch itself, they remain almost entirely presidential in their orientation. The purest cases of this type are the staff agencies of the Presidency, e.g., the Council of Economic Advisers. If the President does not choose to give a staff unit like this any power, then it has little or no influence. Of these agencies it can truly be said that the President is their only constituent, and their power can, therefore, fluctuate a great deal between one Chief Executive and another.

Most agencies, however, do not fall squarely into either of these categorical extremes. They have not formed such strong alliances with outside groups as to become entirely independent of presidential control, nor are they solely dependent upon their position as executive agencies for their vitality. Occupying a middle position, they seek to draw strength from sources inside as well as outside the executive branch. While they would avoid becoming so closely identified with the President as to jeopardize their ties with the legislature, they nevertheless seek to maintain strong lines of support with the White House.

Support is also sought from housekeeping units that have partial control over resources upon which other agencies depend for their operational effectiveness. The Bureau of the Budget, for example, exercises powers that are of vital importance to every other executive agency. The hearings it conducts in the process of framing the executive budget provide a basis for determining how much money each agency needs during the ensuing fiscal year, and this determination by the Bureau usually becomes a ceiling on the appropriations which an agency can expect to receive from Congress. In addition, all agencies must clear their communications with the legislature through the Bureau of the Budget so that the consistency of these communications with the President's policy goals can be checked. The Bureau also has the power to recommend to the President whether he should veto legislation enacted by Congress — legislation which will inevitably affect the fortunes of executive agencies. Finally, the Bureau conducts studies of the efficiency of executive operations which may well lead to reorganization proposals that will greatly alter the power and status of the agencies affected.[23]

Hence, good relations with the Bureau of the Budget are an invaluable asset for any executive agency. Other staff units which also control resources of value to executive agencies include the Civil Service Commission, which administers personnel regulations which

[23] The historical development of these functions of the Bureau of the Budget is traced in Jesse Burkhead, *Government Budgeting* (New York: John Wiley & Sons, 1956), pp. 288–304.

affect an agency's ability to recruit and retain employees, and the General Service Administration, which constructs and operates most government buildings. Of course, in dealing with all these house-keeping units an agency may not be without bargaining power of its own. Aaron Wildavsky's study of the budgetary process shows, for example, that the Bureau of the Budget tends to be generous with those agencies with which it feels Congress will be generous. As Wildavsky puts it: "The Bureau finds itself treating agencies it dislikes much better than those it may like better but who cannot help themselves nearly as much in Congress." [24] An agency's high standing in the legislature may thus be reflected in the treatment it receives at the hands of a staff agency which is presumably responsive to the interests of the President alone — a striking illustration of the extent of legislative influence upon executive behavior.

As far as individual bureaus are concerned, relations with the hierarchy of the department in which they are located is also of strategic importance. While the phenomenon of "bureau autonomy" is widespread in American bureaucracy, there has also been a secular trend toward increasing the power and capacity of departmental officials to control the activities of bureaus under their jurisdiction. Through successive reorganization measures, bureaus have been clustered together in more homogeneous department groupings where they can be subject to more effective supervision; the size and authority of departmental staffs have been strengthened; and legal powers that once resided in the bureaus have been moved upward into the hands of the department.

Moreover, since World War II there has been a steady growth in a new science of management in the public service. Its methods include operations research, systems analysis, the extensive use of program budgeting and cost analysis as a prerequisite to making expenditure decisions, the employment of computers wherever possible in the management process and the establishment of research units to gather information systematically as a basis for policy decisions. These management techniques have greatly enhanced the capacity of departments for overhead control, and have thus had a highly centralizing effect upon the operations of American bureaucracy.

24 Aaron Wildavsky, *op. cit.*, p. 42.

These changes have not affected the power of all bureaus to the same degree, and they have certainly not been uniform with respect to all departments. Moreover, there have been many cross-currents of change which have had offsetting effects. The growth in professionalism in government employment has tended to make many bureaus more specialized, and hence more difficult for generalists in the department hierarchy to control. The activities of natural scientists working at the bureau level are not easily monitored by lay administrators in departmental headquarters units. In addition, bureau chiefs generally have much longer tenure in office than do departmental officials.

The Department of Defense, however, is one agency which has undergone an enormous amount of centralization in recent years. Following his appointment as Secretary of Defense in 1961, Robert McNamara established in the Comptroller's office of the department a cadre of young managerial experts (the so-called Whiz Kids) who quickly gained ascendancy over the military experts in the various branches of the armed forces. In decisions on weapons development and national security strategy, departmental officials were soon able to take over decision-making in fact as well as in form. At the other extreme is a department like Health, Education, and Welfare, where the high degree of professionalism at the bureau level — in medicine, science, welfare, and educational specialties — has long tended to frustrate efforts to establish departmental authority.

The structure of power within the executive branch can thus be looked at from the perspective of the vertical distribution of authority — with attention focused upon either the ability of a President and his staff agencies to influence the decisions and behavior of bureaucrats at lower echelons, or the extent of control which department officials can exert over their own bureaus. Looked at in this way, the executive branch presents a picture today of bureaus possessing a great deal of independent authority, but with a constantly expanding overlay of centralized controls.

It is also possible to look at power in the executive branch in terms of the lateral distribution of influence — between agencies located at approximately the same hierarchical rank but with responsibility for different programs. From this perspective, there are certain possibilities for conflict or cooperation between administrative units, and an agency's success in turning these situations to its advantage will go far to determine its real power or status within the executive branch.

Lateral conflicts between administrative units often arise because these agencies are pursuing goals that are diametrically opposed. The Anti-Trust Division of the Department of Justice, for example, has been in frequent conflict with one or another of the regulatory agencies which administer statutes covering a single major industry within the economy. The division has opposed the merger of business firms when this would seem to have a negative effect on economic competition, while agencies like the Interstate Commerce Commission or the Federal Power Commission have been quite sympathetic to such mergers when they have appeared to promise the emergence of a stronger and more stable industry. Here administrative conflict is a function of a long-standing ambivalence in public policy, because some executive agencies have been charged with promoting economic competition, while others have been allowed to protect selected industries from the hazards and uncertainties of the competitive life.

Inter-agency conflicts are also likely to arise when two agencies pursue goals that are not opposing but closely related. Here conflict occurs for the same reason that it prevails in the private economy — agencies are competitors. This competition may take place in a variety of areas — over questions of jurisdiction, for the support of outside groups, or in the quest for presidential or congressional favor. Competition of this sort has given rise to some of the most celebrated inter-agency conflicts in American administrative history. The struggle between the Corps of Engineers and the Bureau of Reclamation is perhaps the classic case of this kind, as these two agencies have fought for jurisdiction over water resource projects.[25] Similar conflicts have broken out between the Forest Service and the Bureau of Land Management over administration of public lands in the West,[26] and between the Extension Division and the Soil Conservation Service in the Department of Agriculture over agricultural policy.[27]

[25] See Arthur Maass, *Muddy Waters* (Cambridge: Harvard University Press, 1951).

[26] See Norman Wengert, *Natural Resources and the Political Struggle* (Garden City, N.Y.: Doubleday & Co., 1955), p. 52.

[27] See Charles M. Hardin, *The Politics of Agriculture* (Glencoe, Ill.: The Free Press, 1952).

In some areas of policy, agencies administering closely related functions develop a "separate spheres of interest" doctrine as a means of avoiding jurisdictional conflict. Two state universities, for example, may emphasize different educational programs as their chief responsibility, as has traditionally been the case in Indiana, or, as in California, the university and state college systems may serve students with different levels of ability. Of course, the equilibrium produced by this arrangement does not always remain stable. In the period since World War II, state agricultural colleges have almost universally aspired to be full-fledged universities, and this has frequently triggered conflict with the existing state university. "Have-not" organizations, like "have-not" nations, are particularly likely to violate any spheres of interest agreement when an opportunity presents itself to improve their position *vis à vis* a stronger competitor.

The relations between executive agencies need not necessarily be competitive. Since many agencies have common or complementary interests which bind them together, they may establish an informal alliance for the achievement of their objectives. Sometimes agencies, like nations, may negotiate such alliances even though there is a long history of hostility between them. As in international relations, this occurs most frequently when a common danger arises that threatens both of them more than each endangers the other.

For example, in 1944 those life-long antagonists, the Corps of Engineers and the Bureau of Reclamation, were able to arrive at a mutually agreeable arrangement for the development of water resources in the Missouri Valley area. The treaty they signed for this purpose was called the Pick-Sloan plan, and it was forced upon them by, among other considerations, the threat that an agency like the Tennesee Valley Authority might soon be established to take over all water resource activities in the Missouri River area. Labeled by one of its critics as "a shameless, loveless shotgun wedding," this treaty between the Bureau and the Corps helped to dissipate whatever real possibility existed that a valley authority might be given comprehensive jurisdiction over water resource administration in the Missouri basin.[28] Bilateral and multilateral

[28] For an account of the development of the Pick-Sloan plan, see Henry C. Hart, *The Dark Missouri* (Madison: University of Wisconsin Press, 1957), pp. 120–135.

alliances of this sort may often be as essential to an organization's survival as they are to the defense of a nation's security.

Cooperation between executive agencies may also be initiated more formally by legislative or executive action requiring two or more agencies to work together to handle a single program. In state government, for example, it is quite common for programs to be carried on through administrative boards or commissions on which several departments are represented. At the national level, a variety of interdepartmental committees have been established to handle problems that require joint consideration by several agencies for their solution.

In cases of this sort where agencies are brought together as a result of legislative or executive order, the interdepartmental committee in which they are included may become a theater of conflict rather than an instrument of cooperation. In describing national security affairs, where the State, Defense, Treasury, and other executive departments have been yoked together on many interdepartmental committees by the President or Congress, the Senate subcommittee on National Policy Machinery wrote:

> Inter-agency committees are the gray and bloodless ground of bureaucratic warfare — a warfare of position, not of decisive battles. State commonly sees them as devices for bringing "outsiders" into matters it regards as its own, and resists encroachment. The other departments and agencies use them as instruments for "getting into the act." [29]

Formal interdepartmental cooperation that is enforced upon executive agencies may thus serve to mask bitter and protracted warfare between them.

[29] U.S. Cong., 87th, 1st sess. *Organizing for National Security*. Study submitted to the Committee on Government Operations United States Senate by its subcommittee on National Policy Machinery, Jan. 28, 1961 (Washington: U.S. Govt. Printing Office, 1961).

CHAPTER THREE

The Skills
of Bureaucracy

The analysis presented in the preceding chapter might seem to suggest that bureaucratic authority is virtually indistinguishable from political power. From the perspective of administrative politics, an agency's influence in the policy process often appears to depend almost entirely on the constituency strength it commands, or upon its ability to maneuver successfully to advance its interests within the legislative or executive branch of government. To obtain a measure of the scope of an agency's power, it may thus be regarded as necessary only to determine how many followers the agency can muster in its own behalf.

This is not, however, an accurate picture of the bureaucratic role in the policy process. It is not adequate as a description of bureaucratic power in American administration, even though government agencies in this country have very wide-ranging involvements in the political process, and it is certainly not suitable as a description of bureaucracy in Western European government, where, by law and tradition, executive agencies are considerably more insulated from the play of ordinary political forces. Political activity such as the negotiation of alliances with outside groups can be a useful source of power for any administrative agency, but it is by no means the only source of administrative influence.

Of at least equal importance as a source of bureaucratic power is the expertise of executive agencies — the fact that administrators bring to the policy process a wide variety of skills necessary both for making decisions on policy and for carrying these decisions out.

39

This is what Max Weber long ago saw as the distinctive attribute which gave bureaucracy its enormous influence in modern government.

> The decisive reason for the advance of bureaucratic organization has always been its purely technical superiority over any other form of organization. The fully developed bureaucratic mechanism compares with other organizations exactly as does the machine with the nonmechanical modes of production.
>
> . . . . . .
>
> Under normal conditions, the power position of a fully developed bureaucracy is always overtowering. The "political master" finds himself in a position of the "dilettante" who stands opposite the "expert," facing the trained official who stands within the management of administration.[1]

This chapter presents an analysis of expertise as a source of administrative power. It deals first with the sources from which executive agencies draw the technical proficiency which gives them influence upon policy decisions. Secondly, it examines the channels through which expertise is brought to bear in the framing of public policy — the capacity of administrative agencies to give advice to political officials and the discretionary authority vested in bureaucrats to apply expert judgment toward the achievement of policy objectives. Bureaucratic power is thus viewed as stemming in good part from resources peculiar to bureaucracy. It is not simply an extension to the executive branch of processes of group mobilization common to all political activity in a democratic state.

THE SOURCES OF BUREAUCRATIC EXPERTISE

There are a variety of ways in which public bureaucracies acquire the expertise that is so important a source of their power in the governing process. For one thing a large organization is itself a mechanism for enhancing human competence. Men joined to-

---

[1] H. H. Gerth and C. Wright Mills, *From Max Weber: Essays in Sociology* (New York: Oxford University Press, 1946), pp. 214, 232.

gether in complex organizational systems can achieve results that individuals alone could never hope to accomplish — the construction of an atom bomb, the launching of a space vehicle into orbit, or the establishment of an educational system capable of meeting the intellectual needs of all citizens from primary school to post-doctoral training.

Organizations achieve this level of competence by taking complex problems and breaking them down into smaller and hence more manageable tasks. Once problems have been sub-factored in this way, each segment can be handled separately, and then by piecing the parts together, an organization can provide solutions to what may have originally seemed to be insoluble problems. This division of labor within large-scale organizations in addition allows groups of employees to acquire specialized expertise, even though they may not themselves have unusual technical qualifications. It is for these reasons that an organization is itself a source of expertise, quite apart from the skills which its members initially bring to the job.

A second way in which bureaucracies acquire expertise is through the concentrated attention they give to specific problems. Dealing day in and day out with the same tasks gives public agencies an invaluable kind of practical knowledge that comes from experience. This knowledge in time becomes part of the memory of a public organization and is transmitted to new employees by training and indoctrination programs. The task an agency performs may not on the surface appear terribly complex — the cleaning of streets or the removal of snow, for example — but the agency is the institution in society which by experience has come to know the most about it.

The sustained attention which bureaucrats can devote to specific problems gives them a decided advantage in framing policy decisions over political officials who deal with a wide variety of problems and confront each issue of public policy only at sporadic intervals. This advantage is characteristic of both democratic and non-democratic societies. It is perhaps particularly important in the United States because American bureaucrats tend to specialize early and to remain in the service of a particular agency throughout their career. But in European as well as American bureaucracies, expertise reflects continuity in office as well as concentration of energy. Not only do bureaucrats focus their attention on specific problems but they also remain in office for longer periods of time than is customary for politicians.

The knowledge that agencies acquire by continuous attention to particular functions puts them in an especially advantageous position to influence policy when the facts they gather cannot be subject to independent verification or disproof. Intelligence units are especially well situated in this respect. The Central Intelligence Agency, for example, gathers and communicates data to the President that can heavily influence his decisions on foreign policy issues without his having any adequate assurance that the data on which he is acting belong in the realm of fact or fancy. Suppose, for instance, that "central intelligence were to report to the President that there was positive intelligence that the Soviet Union would attack the United States in forty-eight hours, how could he challenge the information? And the dilemma he would face would be particularly cruel because an enemy decision to attack can always be reversed, while a defensive action might, in some circumstances, itself provoke an attack." [2] A monopolistic or near monopolistic control of the "facts" thus provides tremendous reinforcement to the power that bureaucrats possess from specialized and continuous attention to a particular set of responsibilities.

But while organizations have certain inherent assets which contribute greatly to their decision-making skills, it is not these organizational characteristics alone that account for the expertise which is the hallmark of modern bureaucracy. In the modern state this expertise comes pre-eminently from the fact that a variety of highly trained elites practice their trade in public organizations — physicists, economists, engineers — the roster of professions in American society could be called indefinitely without encountering a single skill that does not find extensive employment in one or more executive agencies. And there are several professions such as the military which are only employed in the public service. Moreover, the tendency for professionals to seek employment in public as well as private organizations is on the increase. Etzioni argues that as "the need for costly resources and auxiliary staff has grown, even the traditional professions face mounting pressures to transfer their

---

[2] Harry Howe Ransom, *Can American Democracy Survive Cold War?* (Garden City, N.Y.: Doubleday Anchor Books, 1964), pp. 163–164.

work to organizational structures such as the hospital and the law firm." [3]

Of course not all public organizations exhibit the same degree of professionalism in their employment pattern. Some administrative units like the Post Office Department still hire mainly clerical employees. However, in other agencies, such as the National Institutes of Health, the level of professionalism is very high. Agencies like NIH are in fact often described as "professional organizations" — agencies dominated by individuals whose primary commitment is to the skill they practice rather than the institution by which they are employed.

Agencies which are highly professional in their orientation and employment patterns often occupy a preferred position within the structure of public bureaucracy. State universities, for example, are commonly conceded — by law or custom — a degree of administrative independence not allowed to other public agencies. The same tradition of autonomy ordinarily protects a research agency like the Bureau of Standards from political pressures. When a professional agency enjoys such independence, the influence it exerts in all bargaining situations with other governmental units is greatly enhanced. In the areas in which the standing of public higher education is at its peak, the state university has far more leverage than other agencies with the governor's office, the budget bureau, and legislative committees. It may in fact become virtually a separate branch of government. [4]

In the early history of American bureaucracy, such claims to expertise as administration could make were based largely on the factor of continuity — the clerical employees who then staffed government agencies worked so continuously on particular problems that they acquired a kind of specialized knowledge as an inevitable result. Their expertise had its genesis in their organizational position. And it exacted little deference from politicians. President Andrew Jackson's statement in this regard is often taken as the classic expression of popular disdain for the skills of bureaucracy in early nineteenth-century America: "The duties of all public officers are,

3 Amitai Etzioni, *Modern Organizations* (Englewood Cliffs, N.J.: Prentice-Hall, 1964), p. 77.

4 See Malcolm Moos and Francis E. Rourke, *The Campus and the State* (Baltimore: The Johns Hopkins Press, 1959).

or at least admit of being made, so plain and simple that men of intelligence may readily qualify themselves for their performance; and I can not but believe that more is lost by the long continuance of men in office than is generally gained by their experience." [5]

However, since Jackson's day there has been a sharp up-grading in the skills required to run the modern state. As the innovations wrought by science and technology have increasingly complicated both the environment and the responsibilities of government, the duties of the public service are no longer so "plain and simple" as Jackson once regarded them. Moreover, with the abolition of spoils and the increasing acceptance of merit as the essential qualification necessary for public employment there has been a growing effort to recruit experts to the public service, to provide in-service training programs designed to improve the skills of public employees, and in a variety of other ways to encourage and enhance the development of bureaucratic expertise.

In summary, it can be seen that bureaucratic expertise is rooted in both the characteristics of public organizations and, increasingly, in the skills of their members. Each year the operation of executive agencies at all levels of government demands the employment of a more diverse and complex range of specialized personnel. In sharp contrast to President Jackson's belief in the simplicity of the administrator's task stands the following statement by President John F. Kennedy, delivered in support of an increase in pay for government employees: "The success of this Government, and thus the success of our Nation, depend in the last analysis on the quality of our career services. The legislation enacted by the Congress, as well as the decisions made by me and the Department and Agency heads, must all be implemented by the career men and women in the federal service. In foreign affairs, national defense, science and technology, and a host of other fields, they face unprecedented problems of unprecedented importance. We are all dependent on their sense of loyalty and responsibility as well as their competence and energy." [6]

[5] James D. Richardson, *Messages and Papers of the Presidents* (New York: Bureau of National Literature, 1897), Vol. III, p. 1012.
[6] *Congressional Quarterly Almanac*, 1962, p. 907.

EXPERTISE: CHANNELS OF INFLUENCE

Whether it stems from the characteristics of organizations or the skills of their members, bureaucratic expertise exercises influence over the development of public policy through two chief channels — the capacity of bureaucrats to give advice on policy decisions and the authority they are usually granted to exercise discretion in carrying out these decisions. In the case of advice, the power of bureaucrats is indirect, resting as it does upon their ability to persuade political officials that a certain course of action should be taken. Bureaucrats have influence only if politicians accept their advice. However, once bureaucrats have been granted the right to exercise discretion in the execution of policy, as is common practice in all political systems, their power is direct. The actual content of policy may in some instances become entirely a matter for bureaucratic determination.

The Power of Advice. The agencies in which the power of advice can be seen in its clearest form in American administration are the staff agencies which surround the Presidency, administrative units like the Bureau of the Budget, the Council of Economic Advisers, and the President's Science Advisory Committee. These agencies have little operational authority of their own. They influence policy primarily by influencing the President. The economists who serve with the Bureau of the Budget and the Council of Economic Advisers can shape the President's perspective on fiscal policy, and hence his recommendations to Congress on tax and expenditure measures. The natural scientists who sit on the President's Science Advisory Committee are equally influential with the Chief Executive in the areas of their scientific and technical competence.

The relationship between the President and his advisers at this level of administration involves of course reciprocal benefits. Through their access to the President, professional groups like economists and natural scientists obtain a degree of influence in the policy process they would never otherwise enjoy. The members of most professional groups have neither the time, inclination, nor the capacity to win political office, and involvement in bureaucracy is, therefore, the only avenue to political power open to them.

At the same time, however, the President also derives tangible political benefits from his use of experts. The wisdom of his policy decisions can be greatly enhanced in the eyes of the electorate if he is in a position to assert that these decisions rest on the best professional advice he has been able to obtain. As has been said, for example, of the Council of Economic Advisers: "The acceptance of the Council's expertise as the President's economics increases the acceptance of his authority in matters of economic policy, and where applicable it adds economic persuasion to his strategies of influence. In return, the President provides the principal market for the Council's expertise." [7] The same point has been made with respect to the role of natural scientists in government: "The scientist may find himself on the political firing line, placed there by a politician interested in using the scientist's prestige as an 'expert' to disarm the critics of his (the politician's) choices." [8]

There are risks as well as benefits for the President in his relationship with his advisers. It is, for example, highly important to a President that no one adviser be allowed to exercise monopolistic influence over his decisions. "An executive relying on a single information system became inevitably the prisoner of that system." So writes Arthur Schlesinger, Jr., in describing the elaborate system of checks and balances which Franklin D. Roosevelt maintained to prevent any single adviser from becoming the Rasputin of his administration. "Roosevelt's persistent effort . . . was to check and balance information acquired through official channels by information acquired through a myriad of private, informal, and unorthodox channels and espionage networks." [9]

Roosevelt's method was not, however, foolproof. During World War II, the Joint Chiefs of Staff came to exercise a high degree of influence over his decisions in the field of military affairs: "The mere fact of direct access to the President did not account for the authority of the Joint Chiefs in the conduct of the war. Their power was rather a product of their direct access combined with the

7 Edward S. Flash, Jr., *Economic Advice and Presidential Leadership* (New York: Columbia University Press, 1965), pp. 309–310.

8 Warner R. Schilling, "Scientists, Foreign Policy, and Politics," in Robert Gilpin and Christopher Wright (eds.), *Scientists and National Policy-Making* (New York: Columbia University Press, 1964), p. 169.

9 Arthur M. Schlesinger, Jr., *The Coming of the New Deal* (Boston: Houghton Mifflin Co., 1959), p. 523.

exclusion of civilian advice. . . . Ironic as it was, Roosevelt, who normally skillfully played subordinates off against each other in order to maximize his own authority, allowed one set of advisers to preempt the field with respect to his most important decisions." [10]

One of the chief reasons why Roosevelt was not able to maintain the same balance with respect to military advice that he had earlier established in the domestic area was because military decisions had to be surrounded with so much more secrecy than domestic policy discussions. This requirement of secrecy prevented the use of an open system in which the President could draw advice from as many quarters as he chose: "Wartime . . . imposed secrecy and censorship. No longer could the President look anywhere and everywhere for scraps of information and advice on his preeminent concerns, his most compelling choices. No longer could he pick up any aide or friend he chose to spy out the terrain of his official advisers. His instinct for alternative sources, his avid curiosity, his reach for information and ideas, now had to be confined to men with a 'need to know.' " [11]

In domestic as well as military affairs, a President can overcome some of the disadvantages of dependence upon a closed circle of advisers by relying for advice upon committee structures which permit a broader canvassing of alternatives and even for the emergence of majority and minority points of view between which the President may choose. With a committee a President has some assurance that the advice he is getting reflects pure expertise rather than — as might be the case with a single adviser — professional prejudice or personal idiosyncrasy. C. P. Snow's account of the excessive influence exercised over British Prime Minister Winston Churchill by his scientific adviser, Lord Cherwell, points up this problem.[12]

In American government each of the major advisory institutions in the executive branch — the Joint Chiefs of Staff, the National

[10] Samuel P. Huntington, *The Soldier and the State* (Cambridge: Harvard University Press, 1957), p. 320.

[11] Richard E. Neustadt, "Approaches to Staffing the Presidency: Notes on FDR and JFK," *American Political Science Review*, Vol. 57 (December, 1963), p. 859.

[12] C. P. Snow, *Science and Government* (Cambridge: Harvard University Press, 1961).

Security Council, the Council of Economic Advisers, and the President's science advisory group — is in fact a committee. In the literature of public administration, committees are usually held in low regard as management instruments, since they disperse rather than focus executive leadership and control. But as an advisory institution, the committee has a great deal of utility, and with administrative agencies moving increasingly into the development as well as the execution of policy, committees have become as indispensable for deliberative purposes in the administrative process as they have long been in legislative decision-making.

From the perspective of the President or any agency head who uses an advisory committee, such a group is most valuable if it is under his jurisdiction and owes its primary administrative loyalty to him. Under this arrangement the executive has some assurance that advisers look at problems from his perspective rather than the vantage point of some institutional interest of their own. When the creation of a Council of Economic Advisers was first being considered in 1946, some congressmen tried to have it established as an independent agency responsible as much to Congress and the public as it was to the President. Their hope was that with independent status the agency would become a conservative influence upon the President, as contrasted with the direction in which he was being pushed by liberal economists in his political entourage. This effort to create an independent Council was not, however, successful, and the agency was set up as a staff arm of the Presidency. To be sure, the first chairman of the Council, Edwin Nourse, tried to maintain a position independent of the President, but Council members since that time have defined their role as requiring administrative identification with the President. Their influence on policy has been chiefly a function of the President's willingness to call on them for advice. Worth noting in this connection is the principle long ago enunciated by Machiavelli: "A wise prince, then, seeks advice continually, but when it suits him and not when it suits somebody else." [13]

Of course, an advisory group that is totally dependent upon the Chief Executive for its own survival may be highly reluctant to tell him unpleasant truths he ought to hear. In time the advice a

[13] See *The Prince* in *Machiavelli, The Chief Works and Others,* translated by Allan Gilbert (Durham, N.C.: Duke University Press, 1965), Vol. I, p. 92.

President gets from these experts may do little more than mirror his own opinions. This is likely to be a particularly acute problem when the adviser is a career civil servant whose employment opportunities outside of government are limited. It contributes to candor in the advisory process if advisers are drawn from universities or other outside institutions to which they can return if need be — an option open to the members of both the Council of Economic Advisers and the President's Science Advisory Committee.

The impact of bureaucratic advice upon the policy process stands out very clearly not only in the activities of staff agencies which serve the Presidency, but also in the increasing tendency for the deliberations of Congress to be dominated by "agency bills" — legislation which has been originally drafted in the offices of executive agencies. This administrative initiative in drafting legislation has not received as much attention in recent years as was earlier the case.[14] Analysis of the origins of legislation has focused instead on the increasing role of presidential leadership in the legislative process. Neustadt, for example, carefully documents the way in which the President has established his ascendancy over both the agenda of Congress and legislative proposals emanating from his own executive branch.[15] Of central importance in this development has been the requirement that each agency clear its legislative recommendations with the Bureau of the Budget before submitting them to Congress — a procedure designed to make certain that they are in accord with the program of the President.

And yet this apparent presidential hegemony over the legislative process masks the fact that much of what ultimately comes to be regarded as the President's legislative program stems in the first instance from the advice of bureaucrats in the executive establishment. Located as they are in intimate contact with the everyday processes of government, bureaucrats have an unexcelled vantage point from which to see the need for new legislation. As Lawrence Chamberlain long ago pointed out in tracing the influence of

14 See, for example, *General Interim Report of the House Select Committee on Lobbying Activities*, 81st Cong., 2nd Sess., House Report No. 3138, Oct. 20, 1950, pp. 51–62.

15 See Richard E. Neustadt, "Presidency and Legislation: The Growth of Central Clearance," *American Political Science Review*, Vol. XLVIII (Sept., 1954), pp. 641–671, and "Presidency and Legislation: Planning the President's Program," *American Political Science Review*, Vol. XLIX (Dec., 1955), pp. 980–1021.

bureaucracy on legislation: "The administrative officer lives with his job. In his daily concern with the raw material of administration, at the point where the government and the public meet, he becomes keenly conscious of the inadequacies, ambiguities, and lacunae of the law he administers." [16] The influence of bureaucratic advice thus manifests itself in the process of legislative as well as executive decision.

The Exercise of Discretion. No aspect of the growth of bureaucratic power in this century has been more important than the steady expansion in the scope of administrative discretion. As used in this context, the term "discretion" refers to the ability of an administrator to choose among alternatives — to decide in effect how the power of the state should be used in specific cases. The range of situations in which bureaucrats exercise discretion is virtually boundless. It includes the policeman deciding whether or not to make an arrest, a regulatory agency choosing either to issue or refuse a license or permit, or a selective service board determining whether to draft or defer a particular individual. These decisions may have a vital effect upon the fortunes or even the fate of the individual concerned. Whether or not discretion is, as has been asserted, the "life blood" of administration, its exercise may well have a life or death effect for the individual citizen.[17]

In the traditional theory of public administration in the United States, it was assumed that the administrator's discretion extended only to decisions on means, while the ends or goals of administrative action were fixed by statute or by the directives of a responsible political official. This was the celebrated distinction between politics and administration presented by such early pioneers in the field as Woodrow Wilson and Frank J. Goodnow. This distinction was designed among other things to provide a rationale for insulat-

[16] Lawrence H. Chamberlain, *The President, Congress, and Legislation* (New York: Columbia University Press, 1946), p. 24. For an earlier analysis of the administrator's role in framing legislation, see Edwin E. Witte, "The Preparation of Proposed Legislative Measures by Administrative Departments," in U.S. President's Committee on Administrative Management, *Report with Special Studies* (Wash., D.C.: U.S. Govt. Printing Office, 1937).

[17] See Marshall E. Dimock, "The Role of Discretion in Modern Administration," in John M. Gaus, Leonard D. White, and Marshall E. Dimock (eds.), *The Frontiers of Public Administration* (Chicago: The University of Chicago Press, 1936), p. 59.

ing administrative agencies from exploitation by politicians bent on using administrative offices and powers as the "spoils" of victory at the polls. If bureaucrats did not shape policy, then there was no reason why administrative agencies could not be left in splendid isolation, free to make decisions on personnel, or on administrative organization and procedure, to attain maximum efficiency in carrying on the business of government. As Wilson puts it: "The broad plans of governmental action are not administrative; the detailed execution of such plans is administrative." [18]

This was a highly useful doctrine during the late nineteenth century and early twentieth century in the United States when public bureaucracy was an "infant industry" which needed a protective ideology behind which it could develop. It cannot, however, be regarded as valid doctrine today when the center of power in policy-making has shifted from the legislative to the executive branch and when all bureaucratic decisions are recognized as having at least some implications for policy.

The scope of this administrative discretion is vast with respect to both the everyday routine decisions of government agencies and the major innovative or trend-setting decisions of organizational life. These two broad types of administrative decision have been categorized by Herbert Simon as programmed and non-programmed decisions. In Simon's words: "Decisions are programmed to the extent that they are repetitive and routine, to the extent that a definite procedure has been worked out for handling them so that they don't have to be treated *de novo* each time they occur. . . . Decisions are non-programmed to the extent that they are novel, unstructured, and consequential." [19]

The policy impact of administrative discretion when it is exercised with respect to non-programmed decisions is clear and unmistakable. If the Federal Reserve Board abruptly changes the discount rate, or alters the reserve requirements for member banks to control inflationary tendencies in a booming economy, or to stimulate investment in the face of an impending economic reces-

[18] Woodrow Wilson, "The Study of Administration," *Political Science Quarterly*, Vol. II (June, 1887), p. 212.

[19] Herbert A. Simon, *The New Science of Management Decision* (New York: Harper & Row, 1960), pp. 5–6. *Cf.* also a similar distinction between "routine" and "critical" decisions in Philip Selznick, *Leadership in Administration* (Evanston, Ill.: Row, Peterson & Co., 1957), pp. 29–64.

sion, these are major policy decisions of obvious importance to the society at large. Or the Federal Communications Commission when it sets forth criteria for determining how many television stations are to be allowed in each section of the country is obviously taking the lead in designing a national communications policy through the exercise of its discretionary authority. The independent regulatory agencies as a group have been assigned major responsibilities by Congress for making non-programmed decisions which require "a high degree of expertness, a mastery of technical detail, and continuity and stability of policy." [20]

What is perhaps not quite so clearly apparent is the power inherent in the capacity of bureaucrats to exercise discretion in the area of programmed or routine decision. The fact of the matter is, however, that decisions that may seem merely routine from the point of view of an administrative agency are often of critical importance to the parties affected by these administrative determinations. An individual denied the right to practice a profession as a result of a negative judgment on his qualifications by a licensing board has been grievously affected by the exercise of routine discretion in a situation in which the state controls entry into a profession.

Moreover, a government agency responsible for awarding defense contracts makes vital decisions for industries dependent upon these contracts for their survival, although the decisions may seem ordinary from the point of view of the agency. The exercise of discretion in an area of this kind has side-effects which reach far beyond the business firms immediately affected. The economy of an entire region may be heavily dependent upon the prosperity of a particular industry, and the denial of a defense contract or the closing of a military installation may represent an economic disaster for many communities.

The fact that routine administrative decisions can have such wide-ranging effects for individuals, private organizations, and local communities has led to the establishment of a variety of governmental arrangements designed to monitor these decisions. Individuals subject to the jurisdiction of regulatory agencies are, for example, commonly given an opportunity to appeal a decision ad-

[20] Marver H. Bernstein, *Regulating Business by Independent Commission* (Princeton, N.J.: Princeton University Press, 1955), p. 4.

versely affecting their interests to higher administrative authority. If this review does not lead to satisfactory results, there is in many cases an additional opportunity to obtain a judicial review of the administrative decision. Much of this review procedure rests upon statutory safeguards, such as the Administrative Procedure Act of 1946, or upon the due process requirements of state and national constitutions.

The judiciary is by no means the only outside institution which reviews administrative decisions. In certain areas of national administration Congress has also come to play an increasingly important role in overseeing the use of routine administrative discretion. Real estate transactions by the Department of Defense above a certain magnitude must now receive prior scrutiny by Congress and certain other decisions by administrative agencies must be cleared with congressional committees, including all substantial tax refunds by the Internal Revenue Service to private citizens. Congressional intervention in administrative discretion is largely focused on the areas where large sums of money are involved, where the temptation to administrative corruption is great and where the political side effects may be intense. Since 1964, for example, the Secretary of Defense has been obliged to give Congress thirty days' notice before closing any military installation.[21]

The President himself may find it expedient to monitor the exercise of bureaucratic discretion when it is used in an area of critical national importance. During the war in Vietnam, for example, President Johnson personally participated in the selection of targets for American planes bombing in the North — a range of decision that in other wars was left to subordinate military officials. What this illustration suggests is that decisions which may in one set of circumstances be regarded as routine may in another context take on crucial importance.

An administrative agency can itself go a long way toward controlling the decisions of its own employees through an effective program of internal training. As Herbert Kaufman has shown with respect to the Forest Service, subordinate officials can be so thoroughly indoctrinated with policy goals that the exercise of their

[21] For an analysis of legislative review of administrative decisions, see Joseph P. Harris, *Congressional Control of Administration* (New York: Doubleday Anchor Books, 1965), pp. 226–276.

discretion can be relied upon to mirror faithfully the objectives of the organization. The premises on which their decisions rest have been firmly implanted by a uniform educational background, an effective program of in-service training, and an agency manual that clearly spells out the choices appropriate in particular situations.[22]

But even though there are manifold ways in which the use of discretion can be circumscribed and influenced by other participants in the policy process — political officials, judges, and non-governmental groups — the power that accrues to administrative agencies because of their discretionary authority is still vast. Regulatory agencies, for example, exercise a great deal of power merely because they have the authority to give or withhold benefits, and to inflict or refrain from imposing sanctions. The fact that regulatory agencies have such power forces a group subject to their jurisdiction to defer to them even in situations in which their authority may not be altogether clear. While judicial review of this administrative discretion may be theoretically available, its use in practice may be discouraged by many citizens' fear of suffering unpleasant publicity, or incurring the expense of legal fees, or simply the distraction and delay of litigation.

The history of the Central Intelligence Agency presents countless situations in which administrators have exercised discretion with far-reaching effects on the national welfare. The decision to send an ill-fated U-2 flight over the Soviet Union prior to the summit conference in 1960, as well as the subsidies given to student and other non-governmental groups in the 1950's and the 1960's, provide cogent examples of the ways in which discretionary authority vested in bureaucrats may come back to haunt responsible office-holders.

These illustrations should not, however, lead to the conclusion that the delegation of decision-making power to administrative agencies always has disadvantageous consequences. If this were actually the case, no such delegation would ever occur. The fact is, however, that the exercise of discretionary authority by administrators plays a vital role in protecting and advancing human welfare. Illustrations of these beneficial effects of discretion abound in the daily life of every American community, as public health of-

[22] Herbert Kaufman, *The Forest Ranger* (Baltimore: The Johns Hopkins Press, 1960).

ficials inspect restaurants, fire departments enforce theater safety regulations, and the police attempt to control and prevent traffic accidents. Without administrative discretion, effective government would be impossible in the infinitely varied and rapidly changing environment of twentieth-century society. But the exercise of judgment involves choice, and choice means the formulation of policy. Hence, the high development of administrative discretion in modern society necessarily projects bureaucrats into the center of the policy process.

POLITICS, EXPERTISE, AND POWER

In this and the preceding chapter a distinction has been drawn between the power that administrative agencies acquire through the development of political support, and the influence they exercise as a result of their professional skills. These two sources of bureaucratic power, politics and expertise, while easy to distinguish in analysis, are not as readily separated in the actual practice of executive agencies. More often than not, they are so linked together as sources of influence that it is difficult to tell how much of an agency's impact upon policy stems from the size and strength of its political constituency, and how much rests on the weight of its expertise.

Military officers, for example, are what Janowitz calls "professionals in violence." [23] They have a great deal of influence over the framing of national security policy purely because of their mastery of the art and science of warfare, and of the use of force to accomplish national objectives. Hence their role in the policy process would be strategic whether or not they had any constituency at all. But in modern American society at least, the power of the professional soldier has been enormously enhanced by the formidable network of outside support each of the military services has managed to cultivate. This network includes congressmen and congressional committees with responsibilities in national security matters, industrial firms which are dependent upon defense contracts, and the so-called "back-stop associations" of the military — the Navy League

[23] Morris Janowitz, *The Professional Soldier* (New York: Free Press of Glencoe, 1960), pp. 3–16.

and the Army and Air Force Associations.[24] These and other groups represent the "military-industrial" complex against which President Eisenhower eloquently warned in his farewell address in 1961.

The power of this military industrial complex can easily be exaggerated, since on many issues of national security policy the military point of view has not prevailed, and with regard to specific issues the military usually generates a variety of policy perspectives. But certainly military officers do have substantial influence over the framing of national security policy. What is perhaps impossible to know is how much of this influence simply reflects the pressures of the military lobby and how much springs from deference accorded military expertise itself.

Whatever the relative weight of politics and expertise as sources of bureaucratic power, all executive agencies in the United States recognize the value of political support, and, as illustrated in the previous chapter, devote a great deal of energy to seeking out and nursing a constituency. The extent to which American bureaucracy is thus politicized reflects the fact that a democratic political system was already well established in this country when a bureaucracy of substantial size first began to emerge in the latter part of the nineteenth century. The development of political skills was part of the process by which executive agencies adapted to their environment in order to survive in the egalitarian democratic society in which they found themselves.

This American experience stands in stark contrast to the historical development of bureaucracy in European democratic states. There a highly developed bureaucratic apparatus commonly existed and played a large role in governing the state long before the advent of democratic political institutions. In Europe it was democracy which had to accommodate itself to the presence of a strongly entrenched bureaucratic system. Partly because they enjoyed a security of position that American bureaucracies lacked, and partly because of the conventions of the parliamentary system, executive agencies in European states have historically had less reason and less opportunity to engage in direct political activity of the sort that is so common in the United States.

---

[24] For a close examination of this constellation of interests, see Samuel P. Huntington, *The Common Defense* (New York: Columbia University Press, 1961), pp. 384–404.

But if a politicized bureaucracy is deeply rooted in the American political tradition, so too is a considerable degree of deference to expertise in the governing process. The creation of a variety of political institutions in the United States — including the council-manager form of government in urban communities, the special-authority device in both state and local government, and the independent regulatory commissions at the national level — testifies to the fact that it is very much in the American grain to attempt to de-fuse political controversy by transforming political issues into technical problems. The city and county managers are expected to furnish their local area with professional government based on non-political criteria, and the special authority and the independent regulatory commissions have both been set up to take government away from the politicians and put it in the hands of the experts.

The American political system thus reveals both an extremely high degree of political activity on the part of administrative agencies, and an equally firm commitment to the notion that referring a problem to the bureaucracy takes it out of politics. As a result administrative agencies in the United States are often able to have the best of both worlds. While exhibiting a stance of complete dedication to professional goals, they can simultaneously cultivate as broad a basis of political support as their circumstances will allow. The fabric of their power is thus woven out of both politics and expertise, but precisely in what pattern is often difficult to discern.

However, as a rough generalization applicable to the experience of American national government, it would be fair to say that expertise is the dominant source of bureaucratic authority in the area of foreign or national security policy while bureaucratic politics is much more salient in the administration of domestic activities. In national security policy, the involvement of domestic political groups usually takes place only after a decision has been made. Most decisions are reached in secret, and public opinion is acquainted with what has transpired only through "leaks" — which often come from executive officials who disapprove of what has been decided and are trying to reverse the decision by arousing public opinion against it.

Bureaucratic experts of various kinds thus exercise a pervasive influence over the framing of national security policy. These professional groups include diplomats, military officers, scientists, and what Bernard Brodie calls "scientific strategists." [25] As Huntington describes the development of national defense strategy: "The relative absence of non-governmental groups concerned with strategy enhances the extent and the importance of the bargaining roles of governmental officials and agencies." [26] In this case public participation in actual policy decisions tends to be indirect. The public participates as the officials making the decisions take potential public reactions into account in reaching their own conclusions. While the public is not likely to question the competence of government officials to define the national interest, it is quite capable of eventual resentment against the sacrifices and burdens any international involvement may entail.

In domestic policy-making, on the other hand, a variety of non-governmental groups take a continuous interest in the policy-making processes of administrative agencies. As noted earlier, this relationship is in many instances initiated by the agencies themselves. The views of an agency's public can thus be incorporated into the initial design of policy. In fact bureaucratic policy-making in the domestic area commonly represents a reconciliation of conflicting group interests, as much as it does the application of expertise toward the solution of particular problems.

This distinction between policy-making in the administration of domestic and foreign affairs should not of course be exaggerated. Bureaucrats in the national security area enjoy somewhat more freedom from political pressures in their deliberations. But these pressures are never entirely absent from any area of bureaucratic decision in the United States, so wide and well-traveled are the channels of access between administrative agencies on the one hand and the community on the other.

It is also possible to discern differences in the relative weight of expertise and political activity as sources of bureaucratic power at different levels of government in the American federal system. By and large, administrative agencies in the states and localities are much more intimately involved in the political process than are

[25] Bernard Brodie, "The Scientific Strategists," in Gilpin and Wright, *op. cit.*, pp. 240–256.

[26] Samuel P. Huntington, *The Common Defense* (New York: Columbia University Press, 1961), p. 147.

similar units at the national level. It is still common in state and local government for the heads of administrative agencies to be elected rather than appointed, and this practice inevitably politicizes the atmosphere in which administration is carried on. Moreover, in some of the more backward jurisdictions, patronage is still rife, and agencies serve mainly as auxiliaries for the party organizations. The employees of administrative agencies represent, in any case, a sizable group in state and local politics, and the votes of employee organizations of policemen, firemen, or teachers can easily play a decisive role in local elections.

It is also standard practice for issues as well as offices to be voted upon in state and local elections, and many of these issues are of salient importance to one or more administrative agencies. A school system will lend every effort to secure the passage of a school bond issue on a local ballot, and all agencies face at every election the possibility of becoming involved in a struggle over a public expenditure issue, a referendum, or a constitutional amendment affecting their power or the scope of their activity. However politicized national agencies may be in other ways, they are nevertheless insulated from such election contests. The FBI, for example, while adept at many aspects of political activity, does not, like a local police department, have to concern itself with the success or failure of items on the ballot that critically affect the status of the organization and its members.

There are marked differences in the sources of bureaucratic power not only between national administration and agencies at lower echelons of government but also among agencies at the state and local level. For example, there are many rural states, particularly in the South, where administrative agencies are highly politicized and where little tendency yet exists to develop or defer to bureaucratic expertise. In urban, industrialized states, on the other hand, the professionalization of bureaucracy is often quite advanced, and the operations of administrative agencies have been sealed off from the cruder kinds of political pressure.[27]

[27] For a discussion of these differences between rural and urban states, see Robert B. Highsaw, "The Southern Governor — Challenge to the Strong Executive Theme," *Public Administration Review*, Vol. 19 (Winter, 1959), pp. 7–11, and Joseph A. Schlesinger, "The Politics of the Executive," in Herbert Jacob and Kenneth N. Vines (eds.), *Politics in the American States* (Boston: Little, Brown and Co., 1965), pp. 207–237.

Similar variations exist with respect to local government. From their study of New York City, Sayre and Kaufman conclude that the city's bureaucracies play a key role in its political life.

> Extending the merit system of employment for city employees has had . . . a history of steady and eventually almost complete acceptance in the city's government. . . . The consequences have included not merely the anticipated increase in competence and conventional rationality in the conduct of the city government, but also, and equally significant, the rise of a new form of political power in the city: the career bureaucracies, and especially the organized bureaucracies. Once closely allied to, and greatly dependent upon, the party leaders, the bureaucracies now have the status and the capacity of autonomous participants in the city's political process.[28]

Studies of other cities do not show bureaucracies exerting a comparable degree of influence in the policy process. From Dahl's study of New Haven, it is almost impossible to tell if the city has a bureaucracy, so invisible is it in his account of the governing process of the community.[29] Both Banfield's analysis of Chicago and Jennings' examination of Atlanta assign a more important role to the bureaucratic component in the policy process, but it is still far less significant than that which Sayre and Kaufman depict in New York.[30]

Assuming that these findings are in all cases correct, the strong position of the bureaucracy in the government of New York may be traced to the extraordinary size of the city, and the necessity this imposes for the devolution of authority to administrative agencies. Or the critical factor may be the sharp cleavage between reform and Tammany machine politics in New York's governmental tradition, which led, first, to the practice of giving public agencies strong guarantees in law and custom against political interference, and, second, to the conversion by the bureaucracies of this protection into a mandate for virtually complete autonomy for themselves in the governing process.

[28] Wallace S. Sayre and Herbert Kaufman, *Governing New York City* (New York: Russell Sage Foundation, 1960), p. 732.

[29] Robert A. Dahl, *Who Governs?* (New Haven: Yale University Press, 1961).

[30] Edward C. Banfield, *Political Influence* (New York: Free Press of Glencoe, 1961) and M. Kent Jennings, *Community Influentials* (New York: Free Press of Glencoe, 1964).

In any case, cities differ across the country in the scope of the power which administrative agencies enjoy and in the sources of this power. Parallel differences exist among the states, and between state and national administration. The safest generalization appears to be that the power of bureaucratic expertise varies directly in the United States with the size of the population and the complexity of the environment being governed. Hence, the national bureaucracy is more technically proficient than are, on the whole, state administrative agencies, while the states at the same time are more expert at administration than their own rural units of local government. Cities on the other hand are more likely to have highly skilled bureaucracies than rural states — given the environmental complexity and population expansion which urbanization both reflects and engenders. Hence, as governmental jurisdictions become more urbanized, the need for bureaucratic expertise grows apace, and there is an increasing tendency for the power of administrative agencies to rest upon deference to their expertise as well as upon the cultivation of political support.

CHAPTER FOUR

Differentials in Agency Power

While all administrative agencies have at least some of the political and professional assets upon which bureaucratic power depends, these agencies vary a great deal in their capacity to exercise influence over policy decisions. Some agencies are extraordinarily gifted in their ability to achieve their goals, while others often seem to be step-children of the executive branch. At the lowest ebb of its power, an agency may ultimately come to be "an object of contempt to its enemies and of despair to its friends." [1]

Several factors help to shape these variations in agency power. For one thing, agencies differ a great deal in the strength of their constituencies. Some organizations simply enjoy the support of more influential groups than others or have fewer powerful enemies. The nature of an agency's expertise is also of strategic importance, for not all bureaucratic skills command equal respect in the community. Along with these basic resources of constituency strength and expertise, two other factors are highly instrumental in determining the political effectiveness of an administrative agency. One is an agency's organizational vitality. Because of the nature of their mission or the dedication of their personnel, some agencies generate a good deal more energy than others. The second of these instrumental factors is the quality of leadership with which an agency is blessed. However well-endowed it may be in other respects, an agency that is not effectively led will fall far short of attaining the full measure of its potential influence.

[1] Norton Long, *The Polity* (Chicago: Rand McNally & Co., 1962), p. 50.

While the various factors which help to shape differentials in agency power can thus be sorted out, there is no easy way in which the effectiveness of one source of power can be weighed against another. No common unit of measurement exists for making such comparisons. This is a familiar problem which arises in connection with all efforts to measure power, influence, or authority.[2] It is not, for example, very feasible to use the outcomes of disputes between agencies having apparently different sources of power as a test of the relative value of one kind of power as opposed to another. In the United States at least, the abundance of resources makes it possible to have power contests in which all participants gain at least some of their original objectives. In any case, a single agency may draw power from several different sources, and there is no way of telling how much of an agency's success should be attributed to constituency strength, bureaucratic expertise, organizational vitality, or skillful leadership.

ADMINISTRATIVE CONSTITUENCIES

The most obviously important characteristic of any agency's political following is its effective size. Differentials in agency power are often alleged to rest more than anything else on the number of people an agency serves as well as upon the strategic dispersion of this clientele around the country. In his comparison of the relative influence of the Corps of Engineers and the Bureau of Reclamation upon water resource policy, Arthur Maass traces the superior influence of the Corps precisely to the fact that it provides significant services to a larger and more strategically located constituency.[3] While the irrigation orientation of the Bureau has largely confined its activities to the western part of the United States, where rainfall is often sparse, the Corps performs not only irrigation but also navigation, flood-control, harbor dredging, and other water resource functions which give it a substantial constituency in every section of the country.

The number of congressional districts or states in which an

2 See Robert A. Dahl, *Modern Political Analysis* (Englewood Cliffs, N.J.: Prentice-Hall, 1963), pp. 39–54.

3 Arthur Maass, *Muddy Waters* (Cambridge: Harvard University Press, 1951).

agency's activities are significant often provides a convenient measure of the dimensions of an agency's constituency, where this yardstick can be appropriately used. The power of the Department of Defense in American politics in recent years has often been calculated in precisely this way. Observers have linked the influence of the department with the number of congressional districts in which defense contracts are a significant factor in the local economy. A measure of the department's potential influence in the Senate rather than the House can be derived by identifying the number of states in which domestic industries are heavily dependent upon defense contracts.

Certainly, the size and dispersion of an agency's constituency have a very significant bearing upon the scope of its influence, and agencies are understandably interested in increasing the geographical spread of their clientele. The Department of the Interior, for example, has traditionally been regarded in American politics as devoted primarily to the interests of the West. The department's program heavily emphasizes water resource and public land management activities that are chiefly of concern in the western states, and in deference to this geographical identification the Secretary of the Interior has customarily been selected from the West. More recently, however, with the establishment of the Bureau of Outdoor Recreation under its jurisdiction, the department has for the first time gained an administrative foothold in the metropolitan areas in the Northeast where both the population and the demand for outdoor recreation have enormously expanded. This new constituency gives the department an opportunity to serve substantial population groups in a part of the country in which it has not previously played a significant role.

The breadth of an agency's following is not, however, the sole determinant of its ability to provide an agency with political support. However large it may be, a clientele that is weak in certain other salient respects will not be in a position to give effective political assistance. A small clientele that is highly self-conscious and dedicated to the pursuit of certain tangible objectives which it shares with the agency can in the last analysis be much more helpful than a large clientele that has neither of these characteristics. For example, consumers as a group represent as large a following as any agency could reasonably hope to command and yet agencies

representing consumers have always been notoriously weak in their
political position, primarily because consumers lack self-conscious-
ness as a group, are poorly organized, and generally do not have a
strong identification with agencies set up to serve their interests.

Lack of cohesion on the part of its constituency may also be
highly disadvantageous to an administrative agency. Throughout
much of its early history, the National Labor Relations Board
suffered greatly from the split in the ranks of the trade union movement it was trying to protect between the AFL and the CIO. The
agency often found itself caught in a cross-fire between these rival
labor organizations even while it was trying to fend off attacks from
employers hostile to its very existence.

It might be assumed ordinarily that as the size of an agency's
clientele decreases, its ability to provide the agency with effective
support will diminish. This does not, however, need to be the case,
since a clientele that is dwindling may become, precisely because
it is losing its own position of power in society, even more dependent upon a government agency and the services it provides, and
hence more intensely devoted to it. The intensity of commitment
of its clientele may thus be no less important to an executive agency
than the size and cohesion of its following.

Of course, from the point of view of an administrative agency,
there is no constituency worse than one whose members are not
included within the American voting population. In its successive
incarnations as ECA, MSA, FOA, ICA, and AID, the foreign aid
agency has been gravely disadvantaged by the fact that it serves
foreign groups which do not participate in American elections. In
an effort to counter the weakness, the agency's promotional efforts
have stressed the fact that many American economic interests
benefit from goods produced in this country for eventual shipment
overseas as part of foreign aid.

At the opposite extreme is a constituency such as the agricultural
population which has always enjoyed a position of high prestige in
American society. The view which Jefferson first articulated has
never been seriously challenged in American or for that matter in
any other society: "The proportion which the aggregate of the other
classes of citizens bears in any State to that of its husbandmen, is
the proportion of its unsound to its healthy parts." The most remarkable aspect of this attitude is that it has so strongly persisted

even though each decade has seen a steady decline in the size of the farm population.[4]

Certainly the strong position of the Department of Agriculture in American bureaucracy has not been appreciably weakened by this decline. The ability of the department to maintain its strength even in the face of a sharp contraction in the size of its clientele can partially be attributed to certain traditional characteristics of the American political system, particularly the over-representation of rural areas in legislative decision-making. It also mirrors the prestigious position of the farmer in American life, and the fact that so many urban residents share the farmers' image of themselves as a chosen people.

The structure of a constituency is also important in determining its value to an agency. As noted earlier, an administrative agency that derives most of its support from a single outside group often finds itself excessively dependent upon the group for political support. As a result the group may acquire the power to prevent an agency from pursuing goals that the organization regards as professionally desirable. There is no certainty that the objectives of a bureaucracy will always mesh with the goals of an interest group upon which it depends for political support. Hence, an agency generally prefers to draw its support from a variety of groups, no one of which possesses substantial control over it, while interest groups favor organizational arrangements which enable them to monopolize rather than share membership in an agency's constituency.

As it has been used in this discussion, the term constituency includes all groups that regard themselves or that are regarded by an agency as benefiting from its work. It is, of course, also possible for many groups on the outside to look upon the agency with hostility, or even to desire its extinction.[5] An agency's power thus

[4] The literature bearing on this point is extensive. See, for example, A. Whitney Griswold, *Farming and Democracy* (N.Y.: Harcourt, Brace, 1948), Richard Hofstadter, *The Age of Reform* (N.Y.: Alfred A. Knopf, 1955), and Henry Nash Smith, *Virgin Land* (Cambridge: Harvard University Press, 1950).

[5] Some definitions of constituency include hostile as well as friendly groups within their scope. *Cf.* Matthew Holden, Jr., "'Imperialism' in Bureaucracy," *American Political Science Review*, Vol. LX (Dec., 1966), p. 944. In Holden's view, the constituency of any agency head includes "those who support his ends, those who oppose his ends, and those who wish to intervene for what he regards as 'irrelevant' purposes." Holden also looks upon groups of employees within the agency as "internal constituencies" from the point of view of an

rests on a favorable balance of attitudes toward it in the public. In this respect, regulatory agencies are usually worse off than agencies performing service functions. If it vigorously enforces the law it is charged to administer, a regulatory agency is bound to incur the displeasure of segments of the public upon which it imposes constraints. At the same time, the groups on whose behalf regulation is being carried on may be peevishly critical of the agency for not doing more to advance their interests, or, as often happens, these friendly groups may leave the agency to fend for itself once it has been established.

A service agency, on the other hand, ordinarily generates benefits rather than restrictions upon the public, and the groups it serves usually constitute a solid core of support for the agency's survival and development. Of course, there are great differentials in constituency strength even among such service agencies. Taxpayer opposition to increasing the costs of any program is always possible, and this resistance is not evenly apportioned among all government services. Educational agencies, for example, carry on activities designed to achieve one of the most highly cherished values in American society, and they perform this role for all strata of society. Contrariwise, welfare agencies administer a function that sharply conflicts with the traditional American norm of individual self-reliance, and they perform it for lower-income groups that are unorganized, demoralized and often, as non-whites, vulnerable to racial prejudice. The class as well as the geographical distribution of a clientele may thus be a strategic factor contributing to its influence.

But again, even with respect to a particular administrative function, there may be wide variations in constituency strength among different governmental jurisdictions. A school system in a large urban center may be buffeted constantly about by the conflicting demands of different neighborhoods for better services — a tension which is particularly acute today between white and non-white seg-

---

agency executive. Murray Edelman, on the other hand, defines administrative constituencies as "the groups which have the power to remove the incumbents or kill the organization if it does not respond to their wishes." See "Governmental Organization and Public Policy," *Public Administration Review,* Vol. XII (Autumn, 1952), p. 277. Unfortunately, from their point of view, not many groups served by an administrative agency actually have the power "to kill the organization if it does not respond to their wishes."

ments of the community. In a neighboring suburb, inhabited mainly by well-to-do citizens, the educational system may be at the pinnacle of the administrative pyramid — well financed, the teachers highly paid, and the constituency loyal and devoted to the welfare of the schools.

In summary, it can be said that the ideal administrative constituency from the point of view of an executive agency is large and well distributed throughout all strata of society or in every geographical section of the community. It should include devoted supporters who derive tangible benefit from the services an agency provides. However, an administrative agency should not be excessively dependent upon the support of any segment of its constituency, nor should it carry on activities that threaten the interests of substantial outside groups. Finally, the economic or social activities in which a constituency engages should be in accord with the most highly ranked values in the society. To the extent that it has these characteristics, an agency's constituency is in a position to give it effective support toward the achievement of its goals.

VARIETIES OF BUREAUCRATIC EXPERTISE

While all administrative agencies have some degree of expertise in the functions they perform, not all bureaucratic skills exact equal deference from the community. There are some areas in which the notion of expertise is lightly regarded. Or the amount of expertise available in the private sector of society may equal or outweigh that which a government organization commands. In cases of this sort, a public agency is not in a strong position to use its special skills as a source of influence over public policy.

Where there is a lack of respect for the intrinsic function which an agency performs, the search for clientele support can be particularly intense since a strong constituency is imperative for a public agency whose technical proficiency is not held in high esteem. In such a situation an agency may easily become what Burton Clark has described as a "precarious organization" — constantly obliged to curry public favor in order to survive.[6] In the California adult

6 Burton R. Clark, "Organizational Adaptation and Precarious Values: A Case Study," *American Sociological Review*, Vol. 21 (June, 1956), pp. 327–336.

education program which Clark studied, the administrators involved found it very difficult to adhere to professional standards because of the constant need they faced to satisfy their clientele. Decisions on curriculum and personnel came to be based on student demands rather than professional criteria. As Clark explains it: "acceptance is sought on the basis of service rather than on intrinsic educational worth and professional competence." [7]

As a source of power, expertise reaches its fullest development in those organizations which have skills related to the survival of the society. Scientists and military officers, for example, are in a highly advantageous position today to command respect for their particular talents. Professionals in each of these groups exercise powers that may have "life-or-death" consequences for the citizen. In the case of the military professional, the deference which the public accords may be the product of fear as well as respect, since military organizations alone among public agencies have the capacity to take over physical control of the apparatus of the state.

The ascendancy of military professionals within the bureaucracy seems, however, to be a more pronounced characteristic of backward than of advanced societies. In the so-called emerging nations, the military bureaucracy is in a commanding position in the state because it represents the only well-trained elite and is the most efficiently organized institution in the country.[8] In this context, the military bureaucracy is not subject to effective restraint by either a system of political parties or the countervailing power of civilian agencies. The temptation to seize control of the state is strong, and military coups have, therefore, been a prominent feature of the politics of underdeveloped nations.

In a highly industrialized society like the United States, however, with an extremely well-organized and highly literate population, the influence of the military is offset by that of a variety of other groups and organizations. The military is only one of many skilled professions, and its dominance even in the area of national security policy cannot be assured. The standing of any bureaucratic role is thus shaped in part by the stage of political development a society has reached.

[7] *Ibid.*, p. 335.
[8] See Lucian W. Pye, *Aspects of Political Development* (Boston: Little, Brown and Co., 1966), pp. 172–187.

It also varies a good deal from one period of time to another in any particular society. Prior to World War II, American foreign policy was very much the exclusive preserve of the professional diplomat. Following the outbreak of hostilities, however, the military began to exert increasing influence on foreign policy decisions, and since the war a variety of other skill groups have also come to exercise influence over such decisions. As a result, the Department of State has been hard put in recent years to maintain its hegemony in the field of foreign policy. The skills of a diplomat may be much less relevant to the negotiation of a nuclear test ban treaty than those of a nuclear physicist.

Changes in the state of knowledge play an important part in bringing about these alterations in the status of a particular skill group. The emergence of the new managerial science since World War II — operations research, systems analysis, and a number of other associated techniques — has brought a new group of management specialists to the fore in public as well as private organizations. In the field of military policy these specialists have increasingly come to dominate decisions. Against such software weaponry as "cost-effectiveness" ratios, traditional military tactics as taught at West Point and Annapolis have proved virtually helpless. The heyday of military ascendancy which the Joint Chiefs of Staff achieved during World War II [9] has been succeeded in more recent times by a Pentagon in which civilian strategists have as much influence as military professionals. Many of these civilians are graduates of RAND rather than West Point, and they have provided civilian policy-makers with an alternative source of expertise in wrestling with decisions on national security strategy.

Two characteristics are especially valuable in enhancing the influence of any body of experts within bureaucracy. The first is the possession of a highly technical body of knowledge which the layman cannot readily master, and the second is a capacity to produce tangible achievements which the average man can easily recognize. This combination of obscurity in means and clarity of results seems an irresistible formula for success as far as any professional group is concerned.

[9] See Samuel P. Huntington, *The Soldier and the State* (Cambridge: Harvard University Press, 1957), pp. 317–324.

In the period since World War II, the natural scientists have been the group most strongly exhibiting these two characteristics in bureaucracy. While these scientists may not be quite the "new priesthood" some writers have claimed, still there is no doubt about the prestige and public respect in which the so-called hard sciences are today held.[10] This standing rests in part upon the awe with which scientific wizardry is regarded by the general public, and in part upon the fact that the natural sciences have been — in the areas of their central concern — so extraordinarily successful in obtaining results, whether in the development of nuclear weapons, the exploration of space, or the conquest of disease.

Among social scientists, only economists have achieved comparable standing in recent years in the prestige and influence of their expertise in the framing of public policy.[11] This achievement is most highly visible in the increasing stature of the Council of Economic Advisers — which is charged with chief responsibility for making recommendations to the President on the larger economic issues of the day, such as the maintenance of a high level of employment. But it is also apparent in the increasing use of economic skills in other areas of administration, such as the cost-benefit analysis which is coming to play a dominant role in making decisions on the allocation of budgetary resources among administrative agencies. As is the case with natural scientists, economists' growing power is a result of the specialized nature of their discipline — and the fact that they have demonstrated a capacity to help elected officials make the hard choices which the development of public policy entails.

ORGANIZATIONAL ESPRIT

In recent years, no agency of the national government has ascended more rapidly into the limelight or more quickly won the esteem of all sections of the community than the Peace Corps. Established in

10 For an argument that scientists are in some sense a new "power elite" see Don K. Price, *The Scientific Estate* (Cambridge: Harvard University Press, 1965) and Ralph E. Lapp, *The New Priesthood* (N.Y.: Harper and Row, 1965). *Cf.* also, however, the searching critique of this elitist thesis by Daniel S. Greenberg, "The Myth of the Scientific Elite," *The Public Interest,* Vol. 1 (Fall, 1965), pp. 51–62.

11 *Cf.* the discussion of this point in Harold L. Wilensky, *Organizational Intelligence* (New York: Basic Books, Inc., 1967), pp. 106–107.

1961 to help meet the need of the so-called emerging nations for trained manpower, the agency quickly established itself as one of the major successes of the Kennedy administration. Talented young men and women whose aspirations would not normally be directed toward the public service flocked to the Peace Corps from all directions in spite of the fact that the remuneration they received was meager and the conditions under which they were expected to work abroad were uncomfortable and often hazardous.

What this experience suggests is the enormous value an agency can obtain from the performance of a function which excites the imagination of the community. In an analysis of the structure and operation of bureaucratic systems, Amitai Etzioni identifies three kinds of power which organizations exercise over their members — coercive, remunerative, and normative.[12] Coercive power is the threat or the actual use of physical control, remunerative control is the use of material rewards as incentives, and normative power rests on the manipulation of "esteem, prestige, and ritualistic symbols."

Looked at from the perspective of this analytical scheme, the Peace Corps presents a striking illustration of a normative organization in the public service. Its power rests on the enthusiasm it has been able to generate for its functions from both those who work for it and the community at large. It is not, of course, the only example available of a public agency with this kind of appeal. The Marine Corps and, in its early history at least, the Air Force generated a similar kind of zeal and dedication. Military organizations, with a distinctive tradition and a membership drawn from volunteers rather than conscripts, have traditionally provided the most vivid displays of normative commitment in public bureaucracy. The Peace Corps is an unusual demonstration of the capacity of a public agency to ignite enthusiasm without resort to regimental flags, legends of courage, feats of valor, or the other appeals of military life.

Another way to describe the power of an organization like the Peace Corps is to say that it is charismatic, insofar as it evokes a faith and enthusiasm that transcend rational calculation. However, this use of the term "charismatic" differs sharply from that of Max

---

12 See Amitai Etzioni, *A Comparative Analysis of Complex Oganizations* (N.Y.: Free Press of Glencoe, 1961).

Weber — from whose work the concept of charisma in modern social science is largely derived. In Weber's view, bureaucracy and charisma were antithetical terms. Social movements which began under the leadership of a charismatic leader became bureaucracies as their functions were rationalized and routinized in formal organizations — the sect in the end became a church. "In its economic substructure, as in everything else," Weber wrote, "charismatic domination is the very opposite of bureaucratic domination." [13]

It is possible to discern within bureaucratic organizations themselves a tendency to move from an initial period of enthusiasm and energy to a subsequent stage when the organization becomes routinized and gradually loses a good deal of its original élan. If this transition cannot, in Weber's terminology, be said to mark an evolution from charisma to bureaucracy, it certainly bears a close resemblance to such a transformation. In his description of the "life-cycle" of independent regulatory commissions of the national government, Marver Bernstein shows that once such agencies have gotten past an initial stage of youthful zeal, they undergo a process of devitalization which culminates in old age in a period of debility and decline. "Complacency and inertia appear as inevitable developments in the life cycle of a commission. Although tradition, precedent, and custom can harden into blind routine in all types of social organization, the commission seems to be peculiarly susceptible to the disease of 'administrative arteriosclerosis.'" [14]

This tendency of established organizations to become wedded to routines and resistant to change has frequently been used to justify the creation of new institutions to administer innovative programs. The establishment by President Franklin D. Roosevelt of a variety of "alphabetical" agencies such as the WPA and the CCC in the early 1930's has been widely interpreted as a step on his part to insure that New Deal programs would be carried on with vigor and enthusiasm, rather than being smothered in the red tape and lassitude with which existing agencies would approach their administration.

As far as Roosevelt was concerned, this problem presented itself

[13] See H. H. Gerth and C. Wright Mills (eds.), *From Max Weber: Essays in Sociology* (N.Y.: Oxford University Press, 1946), p. 247.

[14] Marver H. Bernstein, *Regulating Business by Independent Commission* (Princeton, N.J.: Princeton University Press, 1955), p. 101.

in a particularly acute form in the case of the Department of Agriculture. Before Roosevelt's time, the department was strongly committed to a philosophy of confining the national role in agriculture to educational activities channeled through the state extension agencies. The new programs Roosevelt contemplated involved a direct relationship between the national government and the farmer in such fields as rural electrification and soil conservation. Faced with this dilemma, Roosevelt's characteristically diplomatic solution was to establish his programs initially in independent agencies such as the Rural Electrification Administration and the Soil Conservation Service. Then, as these agencies gained sufficient administrative experience and outside political support to insure their viability, he allowed them to be incorporated into the department. By this time the agencies were too strong for the department to sabotage their mission. Indeed, there was on the contrary reasonable expectation that the agencies might infuse the department with their own more aggressive attitude toward agricultural administration.[15]

Organizational esprit depends to a large extent upon the development of an appropriate ideology or sense of mission on the part of an administrative agency both as a method of binding outside supporters to the agency and as a technique for intensifying the loyalty of the organization's employees to its purposes. Some of the conservation agencies have developed almost a mystical sense of mission about their function in the administrative apparatus — the preservation of some priceless asset such as the forests, the soil, natural beauty, or historic monuments. This ideology is a powerful force not only in maintaining the esprit of conservation agencies, but also in heightening their impact upon the development of public policy.

Of course not all agencies perform functions which allow them to develop either a persuasive ideology or a sense of esprit. Any agency may seek through public relations activity to "glamorize" its role, but wholly artificial esprit is difficult to sustain. A great many agencies have a forceful sense of mission early in their history, but tend to lose this crusading spirit as they mature. A few agencies

15 An analysis of Roosevelt's strategy with respect to administrative organization may be found in Arthur Schlesinger, Jr., *The Coming of the New Deal* (Boston: Houghton Mifflin Co., 1959), pp. 533–552.

have managed to sustain it throughout much of their history, and cases of administrative renaissance are not entirely unknown. But where enthusiastic performance is sought for in the public service, the common practice has been to create new agencies in order to achieve it. This is one of many reasons why bureaucracies tend to multiply.

ADMINISTRATIVE STATECRAFT

The role of leadership in shaping the success of any organization is as elusive as it is important. On frequent occasions the ability of an administrative agency to achieve its goals and to secure the resources necessary for its survival depends directly on the identity of its leader. Early in the Truman administration, Congress made it very clear that the Federal Security Agency would never obtain the status of an executive department as long as Oscar Ewing was at the head of the agency. When Eisenhower became President, and Ewing was succeeded by Oveta Culp Hobby, the proposal to transform the FSA into the Department of Health, Education, and Welfare quickly won congressional approval.

The story of Jesse Jones as Secretary of Commerce provides equally impressive evidence of the importance of leadership to an organization. During Jones's tenure as Commerce Secretary, his ability to command support in Congress and devoted allegiance from the business community was legendary. When Roosevelt removed Jones and appointed Henry A. Wallace as Secretary of Commerce in 1945, Congress immediately proceeded to remove from the department one of its most important constituent bureaus — the Reconstruction Finance Corporation. And the decisive factor in bringing about this reduction in the scope of the department's jurisdiction was the replacement of Jones by Wallace.[16]

Of course, in appraising the role of leadership in an administrative agency, it should be recognized that leadership in public administration, like leadership in any organizational context, is to a large extent situational — dependent, that is, on factors in the environment other than the leader himself. Jones was successful as

[16] For a brief but enlightening analysis of Jones's career as Secretary of Commerce, see Richard F. Fenno, *The President's Cabinet* (Cambridge: Harvard University Press, 1959), pp. 234–247.

Secretary of Commerce in large part because his department served a business constituency that was strong in Congress, and still very powerful in the outside community, but that looked upon Jones as its only real protagonist in the executive branch. The influence Jones exercised was thus a product not only of his own capacities but of the circumstances which prevailed when he was in office. For the conservatives in Congress and the country, Jones was a solid and sensible figure in an otherwise radical administration. For President Roosevelt, Jones was a natural bridge to a constituency in which his administration was generally very weak. Jones's personal attributes thus fit perfectly the role he was called upon to play. He would have been far less successful as Secretary of Labor than he was as Secretary of Commerce, since none of his skills could have overcome easily the hostility in Congress and the business community toward the Department of Labor.

In more recent times Sargent Shriver was widely heralded as the model of successful leadership during his tenure as head of the Peace Corps, and many newspaper accounts appeared celebrating the dexterity with which he handled relations with Congress and the public in advancing the cause of the agency over which he presided. However, in 1965 Shriver took over responsibility for the Office of Economic Opportunity — an agency established to carry on "the war against poverty" in the United States. This assignment produced very little in the way of adulatory comment. But the presumption is strong that Shriver was no less able a leader in the Office of Economic Opportunity than he was in the Peace Corps. The critical change that occurred was in the nature of his assignment — from an agency carrying on generally popular activities abroad that did not threaten any important interests in the United States to an agency caught in the turbulence of racial conflict and welfare politics in major American cities.

In short, while an institution is often described as the lengthened shadow of a man, it may be equally correct to say that an executive is the lengthened shadow of an institution, since his own prestige may largely reflect the appeal of the organization he commands. Consequently, an executive who values his reputation as a leader must choose well the institution in which he exercises his talents — to make certain that there is a match between his abilities and the institution's needs. Or better yet, an institution can be one of those rare organizations that so well meets the mood of its time that it is assured of success. But in the end an administrative executive, like Machiavelli's Prince, cannot escape the impact of chance upon the success of his career — being in the right place, at the right time, with the right tactic. As Machiavelli described the fate of leadership: "men are successful while they are in close harmony with Fortune, and when they are out of harmony, they are unsuccessful." [17]

But when this much has been said about the accidental factors which help to determine the success of leadership, it is nonetheless true that executives in quite similar positions in public bureaucracy often have varying degrees of success at their jobs. It seems reasonable to conclude, therefore, that the capacities of a leader can make a difference to an administrative agency and that there are certain skills associated with the effective performance of the executive role in an administrative organization which can be identified as contributing to a leader's success.

Leadership skills in the context of public bureaucracy are of principal value in two areas of an executive's responsibility: (1) externally, in insuring a favorable response to the agency from the outside groups and organizations which control resources upon which it depends; (2) internally, in maintaining the morale of employees of the agency and their commitment to its goals. In large organizations, these external and internal responsibilities of leadership are so complex and demanding that they customarily require considerable specialization, and the organization is in effect run by an executive cabinet in which some individuals are given responsibility for handling external relations, while the duties of others relate primarily to the internal functioning of the institution. However, even under this cabinet system, the head of an agency retains responsibility for the success or failure of the organization, as well as the privilege of choosing his executive associates and of deciding which of his responsibilities he will delegate to them.

As far as the external responsibilities of leadership are concerned, all studies of this subject stress the importance of an executive's ability to create confidence in his own personal and technical

---

[17] See *The Prince* in *Machiavelli, The Chief Works and Others,* translated by Allan Gilbert (Durham, N.C.: Duke University Press, 1965), Vol. I, p. 92.

capacities among those who control resources the agency needs. The executive must be in some sense a "trusted leader" upon whom others can rely. Fenno's work on the appropriations process suggests that the willingness of Congress to grant an agency the funds it needs to carry on its work is very much determined by the confidence legislators have in the head of the organization.[18]

What an agency head needs to know, therefore, is what techniques will help instill confidence in his abilities within his constituency. On this subject we have some guidelines especially in the area of an executive's relations with legislators — a key elite with which the heads of public agencies normally deal. Studies in this field agree that at appropriations hearings and in other contacts with lawmakers, the head of an agency should display such qualities as honesty and clarity in the presentation of his agency's needs, a passion for economy in the use of public funds, and simplicity and affability of manner in personal contacts.[19]

In executive legislative relations, it is essential for an agency executive to recognize that congressmen are in a highly vulnerable political position, subject as they are to removal from office by defeat at the polls. The least the head of any agency can do is avoid, whenever possible, decisions and actions by his agency that may be embarrassing to a congressman in his own district. On the more positive side, he can take steps to lend the congressman certain forms of political support. The agency can routinely provide help and information in handling problems which constituents bring to a congressman, or it may help a congressman advertise himself by arranging for a well-publicized trip to a field installation, or by allowing him to announce from his office the negotiation of a government contract, or the establishment of an administrative facility that will redound to his credit in his district. If reciprocity is the unwritten if not altogether inviolable law of political life, an executive can reasonably expect that these administrative investments will bring a high rate of political return.

As important as any skill an executive may possess is an ability to communicate successfully with his constituency. Very often the

[18] Richard F. Fenno, *The Power of the Purse* (Boston: Little, Brown and Co., 1966), pp. 288–291.
[19] See in this regard *ibid.*, pp. 285–291, and Aaron Wildavsky, *The Politics of the Budgetary Process* (Boston: Little, Brown and Co., 1964), pp. 74–84.

language in which administrative policies are explained and defended is as important to their success as the policies themselves.
In the field of higher education, for example, state university
officials have frequently demonstrated great skill in the use of
metaphors which will bring the distinctive needs of higher learning
home to their agricultural constituencies. In a celebrated defense of
academic freedom, the regents of the University of Wisconsin
stressed their belief that "the great State University of Wisconsin
should ever encourage that continual and fearless *sifting and win-
nowing* by which alone the truth can be found" (italics supplied).
A similar sensitivity to the importance of using appropriate language in addressing a constituency was displayed in Texas where
in protesting efforts to force the university to spend money from
its reserve fund, an administrator vehemently declared that this
policy would deprive the school of its "seed-corn." [20]

In all his relations with his various publics it is important that
an executive not only have the qualities associated with leadership
but that he display these qualities as dramatically as possible.
Victor Thompson has stressed the importance of dramaturgy to the
effective performance of the leader's role.[21] The successful executive must be skilled in impression management — the ability to con-
vey to others a sense of his own capacities. State university presidents
have in recent years concerned themselves not only with being more
efficient but also with convincing others that they are running an
efficient institution:

> it is of vital importance that the state legislature and the tax-
> paying public . . . be convinced of the soundness of university
> operations. Under the pressures of competition from other
> state institutions, a large state university is often forced to put
> on a dramatic show of scientific objectivity in order to justify
> its requests for continued support, even though the dramatic
> props — elaborate formulas, statistical ratios, and so on — may
> have very little to do with the way in which decisions are actu-
> ally made within the academic establishment. As one adminis-
> trative vice-president remarked about the preparation of the

20 Malcolm Moos and Francis E. Rourke, *The Campus and the State* (Baltimore: The Johns Hopkins Press, 1959), pp. 24–25.
21 See Victor A. Thompson, *Modern Organization* (N.Y.: Alfred A. Knopf,
1961), pp. 138–151.

university budget, "We simply use the displays that give us the best image . . ." [22]

As they have developed in recent years in higher education, techniques of scientific management may thus serve not so much to manage the university as to manage the impression that outsiders have about the university.

External relations occupy a good deal of the time and attention of the head of any administrative agency. Just as the duties of the President of the United States have increasingly come to center on foreign affairs so executives in public agencies find themselves drawn increasingly into community relations activity, negotiations with other organizations and a variety of other roles that involve the interaction between their organization and its environment. In the words of Herbert Simon:

> Observation indicates that, as the higher levels are approached in administrative organizations, the administrator's "internal" task (his relations with the organization subordinate to him) decreases in importance relative to his "external" task (his relations with persons outside the organization). An ever larger part of his work may be subsumed under the heads of "public relations" and "promotion." [23]

But if external relations have become dominant in the performance of the executive role, internal responsibilities have by no means disappeared. Apart from attending to the purely housekeeping chores of management, an executive has such major internal responsibilities as arousing the enthusiasm and the energy of the organization's employees for its objectives, settling disputes and conflicts of interest within the organization, and generally serving as a catalytic agent for the continuous appraisal of existing programs, and the inauguration, whenever necessary, of innovations in policy.

Very often these external and internal responsibilities tend to

[22] See Francis E. Rourke and Glenn E. Brooks, "The 'Managerial Revolution' in Higher Education," *Administrative Science Quarterly*, Vol. 9 (September, 1964), pp. 180–181.

[23] Herbert A. Simon, *Administrative Behavior* (N.Y.: The Macmillan Co., 2nd edition, 1957), p. 217.

pull an executive in opposite directions. Decisions he makes to maintain harmony with the outside world may alienate the organization's employees. Conversely, the employees of an agency may push an executive in directions which make it more difficult to maintain good relations with outside groups. While he was Secretary of State, Dean Acheson was a staunch defender of Department of State employees against attacks on their loyalty in Congress — a position which did little to endear him in influential circles of the legislature. On the other hand, his successor, John Foster Dulles, improved his relations with Congress by taking certain steps to tighten security procedures in the department. Since some of these steps were regarded as detrimental to their interests by Department of State employees, Dulles improved the Department's external image at the price of seriously weakening his own standing with its staff.[24]

Hard choices of this kind confront an executive at every turn — the need to balance uncertain gains against certain losses, or perhaps to choose the lesser of two evils in a context in which the question of which is the lesser evil is precisely the issue in doubt. In the case of national agencies, an executive is confronted by a board of directors in the form of a congressional committee which has many members who — for partisan reasons — wish him ill rather than well. The President whom he nominally serves may well abandon him if he gets into trouble. The agency's employees are career bureaucrats who may choose to ignore or defy him, and who cannot easily be disciplined or dismissed. It is in this refractory environment that administrative statecraft must be carried on in the public service, and what is perhaps most remarkable is not that many fail, but that some succeed.

THE PURSUIT OF POWER

If the sources of administrative power are varied, so too are the motives which animate administrative agencies in their quest for primacy. Most clearly apparent is the desire of agencies to strengthen

---

[24] See in this regard Norman A. Graebner (ed.), *An Uncertain Tradition: American Secretaries of State in the Twentieth Century* (N.Y.: McGraw-Hill, 1961), pp. 267–308.

their position to enhance their ability to achieve such manifest goals as better medical care, a more effective system of crime control, or the prevention of water pollution. The statutory objectives of public agencies today are wide-ranging, and in order to fulfill its mission, every agency requires an adequate supply of resources to employ personnel and meet the other expenses of organizational life. These resources are easier for the strong to obtain than the weak, so power is sought not for its own sake but because it is an essential prerequisite for carrying on an effective program.

But along with these manifest goals by which agencies are inspired in their quest for power, certain other latent objectives are also commonly present. At the upper reaches of the hierarchy, agency executives may have a strong desire for power as a means of gratifying a personal need for status and the other perquisites of office. On the part of rank-and-file personnel, the pursuit of power may be primarily designed to insure the continuation of certain more tangible rewards which are important to them as civil servants, including adequate salaries, pensions, working conditions, and fringe benefits. The preservation and improvement of these remunerative incentives have become the special responsibility of public employee organizations.[25]

These varied motives for which power is sought are not, of course, necessarily incompatible. An agency may be most capable of serving the public interest when it is led by an ambitious chief executive, who may, while using the agency as a springboard for advancing his own career, bring it to new levels of achievement in its capacity for public service. A private vice can, as Adam Smith long ago noted, often be transformed into a public virtue. The community may also be as well served if rank-and-file employees are allowed to gratify their continuing desire for improvements in remuneration and working conditions. There are certainly reasonable grounds for believing that satisfied employees will be more efficient than those who cherish grievances. Public and private

---

[25] The divergence between the goals of individuals and the goals of the organizations of which they are members is a recurring theme in organization theory. See especially the work of Chris Argyris, *Personality and Organization: The Conflict Between System and the Individual* (N.Y.: Harper, 1957), and *Interpersonal Competence and Organizational Effectiveness* (Homewood, Ill.: Dorsey Press, 1962).

interests may thus dovetail neatly together, in the best of all possible administrative worlds.

There are, however, other less attractive possibilities. The personal goals of agency employees may gain a distinct priority over the actual purposes for which the agency was created. This distortion occurs in its worst form in cases of administrative corruption, where some members of a law enforcement agency, for example, look upon its power not as a means of protecting the safety of the public, but as an instrument for extorting tribute from the individuals engaged in the illegal activity they are supposed to be suppressing. In situations of this kind, the needs of the public recede altogether, and administrative power is sought merely to advance the private goals of agency employees.

Of course, the private interests which members of an administrative agency serve need not necessarily be their own. As noted earlier, there are many public agencies which, either in their initial establishment or eventual development, exist mainly as satellite organizations for outside groups. A licensing board, for example, may be set up for the manifest public purpose of insuring that certain professional standards are adhered to in the practice of a particular skill. But in actual fact the latent function of such an agency may be that of limiting entry into the profession to protect the economic position of present members of the group, thus inflicting costs upon the public it is supposed to serve.

Less obvious but no less difficult are the cases in which public organizations are in a position to justify their pursuit of power on the basis of disinterested criteria such as service to the public, when in point of fact, power is sought only to advance the interests of the organization's members. In this category would be pessimistic assessments by the armed forces of a potential enemy's capabilities and intentions which are contrived in order to pressure the public into supporting an expansion in the strength of the military.

Whatever its motives may be in seeking greater authority, an agency must constantly reckon with the fact that an expansion in jurisdiction does not always result in an expansion in power. While bureaucracies are often pictured as being implacably imperialist in their desire to expand their jurisdiction, in actual fact there are occasions when an agency may increase its power by narrowing, or refusing to expand, the scope of its legal authority. According to

Sayre and Kaufman, for example, the agencies in New York City's government

> . . . compete to avoid program assignments that are especially difficult and controversial. The Commissioner of Hospitals. and the Commissioner of Correction have both tried to prevent lodging responsibility for treatment of narcotics addicts in their departments, and the Department of Health has been restive under burdens of building inspection the Commissioner and the Board of Health would generally prefer to have placed entirely on the Department of Buildings.[26]

Thus, in the quest for power an agency's strategy has to be one of optimizing rather than maximizing its jurisdiction. Activities that have weak political support, are inordinately expensive, or that divert an agency from its essential purposes represent liabilities rather than assets from the point of view of an agency's power balance.

Perhaps the most embarrassing kind of jurisdiction an agency can acquire is control over an activity that is anathema to its own constituency. This was the unhappy fate of the Department of Labor in 1963, when it was put in charge of administering the Landrum-Griffin Act, a statute designed to protect union members from abuses of power by their own officers. Prior to its enactment this legislation had been bitterly fought by the labor organizations that represent the department's chief source of outside support, and since 1963 the Department of Labor has discharged its responsibilities in this area with a notable lack of enthusiasm.[27] In cases of this kind, administration of the law may become in fact nullification of the law, or, as some would put it, sabotage of its intent.

It should be borne in mind that executive agencies, like all contestants in the struggle for power, operate with imperfect knowledge regarding the kinds of strategy that will advance their interests. An agency may, for example, strongly resist measures which it feels will reduce its authority, only to find, when the changes actually take place, that no such effects have occurred. In advancing or

[26] Wallace S. Sayre and Herbert Kaufman, *Governing New York City* (N.Y.: Russell Sage Foundation, 1960), p. 262.

[27] A similar case involving the failure of the Federal Power Commission to enforce the Natural Gas Act is cited by Holden, *op. cit.*, p. 945.

protecting its power interests, as on other matters, an executive agency thus operates within the limits of what Herbert Simon calls "bounded rationality." [28] The course of action best calculated to achieve its objectives is not always clear to it.

28 See Herbert Simon, *Models of Man* (New York: John Wiley & Sons, Inc., 1957), pp. 196–206.

Part Two

BUREAUCRACY AND PUBLIC POLICY

CHAPTER FIVE

The Policy Process in Bureaucracy

The preceding chapters have examined some of the principal reasons why administrative agencies now exert such great influence upon public policy. The basic resources upon which administrative power has been shown to depend are the support of an influential constituency and the possession of a skill essential to reaching decisions in vital areas of policy. If politics is a source of bureaucratic power, so too is knowledge. An agency's ability to exert influence in the policy process can also be traced to the esprit or vitality of the organization and the extent to which it is effectively led. In the most powerful of administrative organizations, such as the Federal Bureau of Investigation, a position of influence tends to reflect the simultaneous presence of all these factors — strong public support, a valued skill, organizational esprit, and adroit leadership.

In this chapter we begin a consideration of some of the essential characteristics of the policy-making process in bureaucracy. Two problems are of central importance in this analysis of the forces and factors which shape the outcome of deliberations on policy issues within administrative agencies. The first is the identity of the principal groups in administrative agencies which participate in the development of policy. Internal administrative politics, in the sense of conflict among individuals playing different roles inside executive agencies, do as much to shape the structure of policy as the interaction between agencies and outside groups and organizations.

The second question at the center of concern is the nature of the policy process within administrative agencies. In terms of both its effectiveness and its consistency with democratic norms, how does policy-making change when its center of gravity shifts from legislative assemblies to the corridors of bureaucracy? The chapter concludes with an examination of some of the significant ways in which the policy-making process in executive agencies is shaped by the fact that it is being carried on within a bureaucratic environment.

PARTICIPANTS IN BUREAUCRATIC POLICY-MAKING

In much of the literature and folklore about bureaucracy, the image that emerges is one of unity in structure and uniformity in perspective. Generalizations about the bureaucrat and the administrative role in government often seem to assume a total homogeneity in outlook on the part of all bureaucrats. By outside observers, the word most often used to describe bureaucratic organizations is "monolithic."

Viewed from within, however, a far different picture emerges. A government agency, like any large and complex organization, can be seen to embrace a variety of points of view which produce diversity in perspective and often generate sharp disputes within the inner councils of the agency. Like a family or any other social organization that radiates an image of togetherness to the outside observer, an executive agency shows itself upon close inspection to be far from uniform in the attitudes and behavior of its members.

More specifically there are three basic cleavages in the ranks of bureaucracy which are central factors in the development of policy within administrative agencies. In the first place, there may be a sharp difference in the role and attitude of political officials at the top of the administrative pyramid and the career administrators beneath them. Secondly, within the ranks of career employees themselves there is frequently a wide divergence in outlook between the professionals who employ the skills with which the organization serves the community, and the administrators whose chief function is that of maintaining the organization in existence. Finally, there is a possibility for "lateral entrance" into an agency's policy deliberations on the part of outside experts who play an advisory or consultative role, or even for temporary periods, may serve in a full-time capacity with the agency. These outsiders commonly represent a quite distinctive force in the framing of bureaucratic policy.

Political Executives and the Career Staff. A relationship which is fundamental to the determination of policy in any governmental bureaucracy is the interaction between political executives at the top of the administrative pyramid and career officials subordinate to them. In a democratic state the political executive usually represents the political party which has been victorious at the polls. In non-democratic societies he represents the ruling group that presides over the destinies of the state. And in both democratic and non-democratic states, the task of preserving a stable balance between political and career officials is a continuing source of difficulty in framing governmental policy.

The traditional interpretation of the relationship between the political and the career administrator stresses the superior influence of the career official upon policy decisions. Max Weber, for example, contends that "the absolute monarch is powerless opposite the superior knowledge of the bureaucratic expert — in a certain sense more powerless than any other political head. . . . The Russian czar of the old regime was seldom able to accomplish permanently anything that displeased his bureaucracy and hurt the power interests of the bureaucrats." [1] A similar view was expressed by John Stuart Mill: "Where everything is done through the bureaucracy, nothing to which the bureaucracy is really adverse can be done at all." [2]

In American bureaucracy, however, the relationship between political and bureaucratic officials is far more subtle and complex than the comments of either Weber or Mill might suggest. While the career official has certain advantages in this relationship, including continuity in office and a greater familiarity with the work of the agency, the political executive is far from powerless. For one thing he presides over a hierarchical system in which his office is a primary source of legitimate authority. Consequently, there is a

[1] H. H. Gerth and C. Wright Mills, *From Max Weber: Essays in Sociology* (New York: Oxford University Press, 1946), p. 234.

[2] John Stuart Mill, *On Liberty* (New York: Appleton-Century-Crofts, 1947), p. 115.

strong tendency for career bureaucrats to tailor their recommendations to fit what are believed to be his views on policy. And once
he has made up his mind on a policy question, these officials will
ordinarily support his decision, even if they disagree with it. The
cases in which career subordinates have openly repudiated the
decisions of their political superiors are notorious — the Glavis-
Ballinger dispute,[3] for example — but they are nonetheless excep-
tional. More common is the willingness of bureaucrats to go along
with policies decided upon at a higher level.

When opposition manifests itself, it is more likely to be covert
than open — guerrilla warfare rather than a frontal assault. Career
officials will confide their doubts regarding the wisdom of the policies being followed by their political superiors to friendly congressmen or reporters, or they may alert pressure groups with which
they have an intimate relationship. Using these tactics, the postal
employee organizations have often been successful in defeating proposals of departmental officials which they regarded as jeopardizing
their own job security: "postal employee organizations can turn congressional mail on and off in terrific volume within 24 hours, and the
number of letters can be formidable."[4] During the Vietnam war,
the Armed Forces repeatedly used testimony before the Senate Pre-
paredness Subcommittee as a means of getting their disagreements
with the Secretary of Defense before the public eye.

Career bureaucrats thus tend to convert disputes with political
executives into conflicts between their superiors and outside organizations. In this way, they can pursue their objectives without jeop-
ardy to the forms of bureaucratic life or the safety of their own
position. Moreover, by avoiding an open break with their superior,
they can continue to pass ammunition to his critics from the
security of their intimate participation in the affairs and deliberations of the agency. In this surreptitious way, career officials can
incite political conflict in the outside world without themselves
participating in the combat.

Such warfare is not a frequent occurrence. More commonly, the
relationship between political executives and career officials can be

3 See Harold Stein, (ed.), *Public Administration and Policy Development* (New
York: Harcourt, Brace, 1952), pp. 77–87. This dispute centered on the campaign
waged by a subordinate official in the General Land Office against the policies
being followed by his superiors in disposing of public land.

4 Marver Bernstein, *The Job of the Federal Executive* (Washington, D.C.:
The Brookings Institution, 1958), p. 99.

described in Lindblom's term, as one of "mutual accommodation." [5] Career subordinates have good reason for deferring to their political superior. As already noted, he is invested with the authority of office in a bureaucratic environment in which rank is an impressive symbol of power. Congressmen may be prepared to treat departmental executives with familiarity if not contempt. Ordinary bureaucrats are not.

Secondly, the political executive, whether elected or appointed, is in some sense a symbol of public control of the governmental process. In a society as impregnated with democratic ideology as the United States, this is a formidable source of authority. Finally, in addition to representing the authority of the community in the agency, the political executive also represents the agency in the community. Bureaucrats cannot publicly undermine him without risking injury to the organization with which their personal fortunes are linked. He is the best salesman they have for the achievement of the agency's goals and the replenishment of its resources.

At the same time political executives cannot run roughshod over the views of their career subordinates. While they may be able to coerce these subordinates into obedience, they certainly cannot force them into the enthusiastic performance of their duties which is essential if the agency is to attain a high level of effectiveness. Moreover, the capacity of career subordinates to make trouble for the executives in the outside community is, as has been suggested, not insubstantial, and this threat also calls for the exercise of diplomacy by the political executive in his dealings with these officials. Such diplomacy may sometimes lead a chief executive to call for improvements in salary and fringe benefits for his staff as a means of purchasing their support for his own policy goals.[6]

In the formal theory of public administration, the role of the

[5] See Charles E. Lindblom, *The Intelligence of Democracy* (New York: The Free Press, 1965). A study of the attitudes of career officials toward political appointees showed that these appointees are generally held in high esteem. See M. Kent Jennings, Milton C. Cummings, Jr., and Franklin P. Kilpatrick, "Trusted Leaders: Perceptions of Appointed Federal Officials," *Public Opinion Quarterly*, Vol. 30 (Fall, 1966), pp. 368–384.

[6] However, as noted on p. 82, an agency executive often has to tread a tightrope in wooing his subordinates without alienating important constituency groups. In contemporary urban politics, for example, a police commissioner faces the difficult task of handling the "police brutality" issue to satisfy both the members of his own department and civil rights organizations in the city.

career staff is regarded as primarily that of ensuring competence in
the design of policy — the techniques used to achieve goals should
be the most effective available. In actual practice, however, the
career staff also tends to develop a fine sensitivity to the political
pressures to which an agency is subject. A political executive's best
advice on how to operate politically may well come from his career
subordinates. They know their way around the political thickets
which surround the agency; he does not. Moreover, legislators tend
to seek advice on policy questions from career officials, since they
often regard these officials as more knowledgeable and trustworthy
than political executives.

On the other hand, it is not infrequent today for the politically
appointed head of an executive agency to have at least as much if
not more competence in the agency's area of expertise than his own
career staff. This was certainly the case in the Kennedy administration when Francis Keppel, dean of the Harvard Graduate School
of Education, became head of the U.S. Office of Education, or when
Glenn Seaborg, a Nobel laureate in physics, took over as chairman of
the Atomic Energy Commission. In situations of this sort, the
political appointee's chief role may be that of providing professional guidance in policy development, while the career officials
help him avoid political pitfalls in his dealings with the community, Congress, and other executive agencies.

In democratic societies at least, it has traditionally been assumed
that public policy should reflect both the needs and desires of
citizens, and the application of the best expert advice and technical
skill in satisfying these aspirations. The conventional wisdom has
been that the role of reflecting popular preferences should be played
by political executives, while career civil servants provide whatever
expertise is needed to achieve policy goals. This is the arrangement
to be found in British governmental structure, and it has been en-
dorsed by a number of official studies and reports on the American
system.[7] As has been indicated, however, bureaucracy in the United

7 See, for example, U.S. Commission on Organization of the Executive Branch
of the Government, *Task Force Report on Personnel and Civil Service* (Washington: U.S. Government Printing Office, 1955). In its final report the Commission recommended that career administrators be relieved "of responsibility
for advocacy or defense of policies and programs" and "kept out of direct participation in political controversies." See *Personnel and Civil Service:* A Report
to the Congress by the Commission on Organization of the Executive Branch
of the Government (Washington: Government Printing Office, 1955), p. 29.

States tends not to follow this neat division of labor. Career officials are often astute politicians and political executives may have impressive credentials as experts. But it has certainly not been demonstrated that policy decisions in American bureaucracy are any less responsive or less competent because the actors involved do not always play the roles assigned to them.

Professionals and Administrators. In a growing number of organizations, in the public service as well as in private life, an increasingly strategic role is being assumed by so-called professional employees — individuals with highly developed skills whose commitment to an organization arises primarily from the fact that it gives them an opportunity to practice their specialized craft.[8] Their primary loyalty remains, however, to their own profession, not to the organization, and their attitudes on many questions are formed by and sometimes peculiar to their particular discipline. Many professions in the public service — city planners, foresters, social workers, and others — have a distinctive ideology with respect to policy in their own area of concern that springs from a deeply rooted tradition of looking at problems in a certain way.

City planners, for example, have a profound commitment to the importance of a city's having a comprehensive design for its own development to which specific proposals for urban land use can be related. Social workers often have a similar attitude of dedication toward the necessity of taking care of the poor and underprivileged in society — an attitude which, at least in its intensity, sets them apart from other groups in bureaucracy. Foresters, like other conservationists, have an almost mystical reverence for the natural resources under their jurisdiction. A founding father of a profession, such as Gifford Pinchot in the case of forestry, may have a place of honor in its development not unlike that of the first patriarch of a religion. Like a religious sect a profession may also have its hallowed martyrs. Billy Mitchell, in the case of the Air Force, is one notable example. J. Robert Oppenheimer, in the case of the scientific community, is another.

8 For an illuminating discussion of the role of the professional in organizations, see Amitai Etzioni, "Authority Structure and Organizational Effectiveness," *Administrative Science Quarterly*, Vol. 4 (June, 1959), pp. 43–67. An analysis of the attitudes and behavior of professionals in more specifically governmental organizations may be found in John J. Corson and R. Shale Paul, *Men Near the Top* (Baltimore: The Johns Hopkins Press, 1966), pp. 77–102.

There is, however, another group of employees within executive agencies whose work is also essential to their successful operation. The role and perspective of this group, here described as administrators, is shaped by the organization in which they function, not by any craft or skill in which they specialize. Within public bureaucracy there are two particularly vital tasks which such administrators perform. The first is that of attending to certain auxiliary functions which are indispensable to the operation of any organization, such as the handling of funds and the maintenance of physical plant and equipment. The second, and more prominent, role is that of coordinating the work of professionals within the organization and establishing effective liaison with the community. These latter tasks have pushed administrators into positions of executive leadership in a good many organizations.

Policy as it develops within executive agencies — and within the government itself — is heavily influenced by pulling and hauling between professional and administrative points of view. Professionals are primarily committed to the attainment of the goals that their skill is designed to achieve. Administrators, if their function is that of providing staff services, are likely to emphasize economy in the use of resources. This is, for example, the common perspective of budget officers and purchasing officials. In a dichotomy of this sort, the concern of professionals is with the effectiveness of policy — the achievement of objectives no matter what the cost. Fiscal administrators, on the other hand, are principally concerned with efficiency in the use of the organization's assets — attaining results with a minimum expenditure of scarce resources upon which there are multiple claims within the organization.[9]

Administrators with more general responsibilities in executive or public relations capacities are likely to be far more sensitive than professionals to the need for compromise in pursuing objectives — the necessity of settling for half-a-loaf, or of taking the views of other groups and organizations into account in reaching decisions. Such administrators are a force for moderation in the policy process. The qualities needed in this kind of administrative role

---

[9] *Cf.* the distinction between efficiency and effectiveness in Amitai Etzioni, *Modern Organizations* (Englewood Cliffs, N.J.: Prentice-Hall, 1964), pp. 8–10. Herbert Simon, *Administrative Behavior* (New York: The Macmillan Co., 2nd edition, 1957), presents a similar contrast between "efficiency" and "adequacy."

are a gift for negotiation and diplomacy, which stands in rather stark contrast to the fanatical zeal with which professionals frequently advocate their distinctive point of view.

In looking at the development of policy within administrative agencies, it is clear that a great deal of the energy and innovative force in the policy process comes from professionals. True enough, the perspective of professionals is often narrow. They commonly have difficulty in seeing a problem in its full breadth and complexity from the confines of their own specialty. Moreover, the inability of professionals to take costs into adequate account in the pursuit of policy goals, or to follow lines of authority and orderly procedure, is often a source of confusion and conflict within organizations.

But in the end it is professionals who are at the growing edge of policy. It is their skills which give agencies their problem-solving capacities; and their specialty often gives them foresight into the shape of things to come. Returning to the religious analogy, professionals frequently play the role of prophet in the policy process — seeing beforehand problems that lie far ahead. Scientists in such fields as nuclear energy, weapons development, and space exploration have been able to perform precisely this kind of prophetic function in recent years in the development of national science and defense policy.

The importance of their own role often leads professionals to disparage the contribution that administrators can make to an executive agency. From the professional's perspective, the administrator is often looked upon as merely a bookkeeper or, that ultimate insult, a "paper-shuffler." The professional commonly regards administrative rules and procedures which are designed to promote organizational efficiency as stifling to both energy and imagination. Generally, professionals believe that organizations should be subject only to loose and flexible supervision, rather than the tight rein of control that administrators characteristically prefer.

> Irritation over the approval of travel is typical of the administrative "tight rein" against which professionals often rebel. They complain that such controls consume time they should be spending on professional work. One regarded the review of scientific positions (required by the personnel

officer) as "a waste of time." . . . Still another professional
complained of the requirement that he make out officer fitness
reports. "[I] do not regard this type of report as relevant to
the functions of a scientific research organization." [10]

The stereotyped image of the professional in the eye of the
administrator may be no less unflattering. Administrators in many
agencies tend to look upon their role as primarily that of formulat-
ing policy with a realism and breadth of perspective that professionals by themselves could never provide. While these two contrasting
outlooks engender tension and often conflict within executive
agencies, both professionals and administrators have a vital and
complementary role to play in the development of policy. If professionals provide such useful ingredients as imagination and
technical skill, administrators can help insure that policy attains
maximum results with the resources available, and that it is sensitive to the needs and interests of the community groups which will
be affected by it.

This latter consideration is particularly important, since professional groups habitually frame programs in areas for which they are
responsible in ways that may be more advantageous to themselves
than to the groups affected by these policies. Administrators in city
hospitals can represent patients or their families in the development
of policies governing medical care, and at state universities administrators can play a similar role in seeing that courses and schedules
are designed with the interests of the student as well as the professor
in mind.

The split between professionals and administrators has been
examined here primarily as it operates between groups playing
different roles within executive agencies. However, this cleavage in
viewpoint can also characterize the relations between agencies. In
the national government, for example, agencies that employ a high
percentage of professional employees, such as the National Science
Foundation, the National Aeronautics and Space Agency, and the
National Institutes of Health, have a highly professional outlook
which can generate sharp disagreement with an agency like the

[10] Corson and Paul, *op. cit.*, pp. 90–91. This disparity in attitudes between
professionals and administrators is also discussed in Francis E. Rourke, "Bureaucracy in Conflict: Administrators and Professionals," *Ethics*, Vol. LXX (April,
1960), pp. 220–227.

General Services Administration which is, by way of contrast, thoroughly administrative in its orientation.

Of course, disparity in viewpoint between two professionalized agencies is equally possible. It is in fact such disagreement which provides the *raison d'être* for one of the most important of administrative roles — the mediation of conflict between professional groups. Even in the United States, resources are not unlimited and priorities have to be established. Since all professional groups would regard the needs of their own area of concern as having first claim in any allocation decision, the role of the administrator in helping to determine the order in which needs will be met is a strategic source of influence over public policy. It is perhaps the greatest paradox of the policy-making process within bureaucracy that professionals, who have such great influence when program objectives are being determined, have so much less power over the allocation of the fiscal resources which enable objectives to be realized.

Bureaucracy: Insiders and Outsiders. In the United States today, it is possible for many individuals with a high standing in, for example, one of the scientific professions to participate directly in the process of policy-making within executive agencies without committing themselves to full-time government employment. This is evident especially, but not exclusively, in the case of university scientists who can retain positions in private life while having a voice in the development of policy within the inner councils of public bureaucracy.

Commonly, the outsider gains this entree by serving in an advisory capacity to a government agency. The members of the President's Science Advisory Committee are drawn almost entirely from private life, as is the membership of innumerable lesser committees which help the National Science Foundation and other agencies make governmental decisions on fellowships, the support of research projects, and the location of new laboratory facilities. In many cases, the scientists thus serving as advisers have considerably greater eminence in their own professions than scientists who are full-time government employees. As a result, these outside scientists tend to be deferred to on policy questions by their professional colleagues in the executive agencies in which they are jointly associated.

Outsiders holding advisory positions within bureaucracy have been at the center of some of the most celebrated policy disputes that have arisen within the national government since World War II. The struggle over the question of whether the United States should attempt to develop a hydrogen bomb had its focus in the General Advisory Committee to the Atomic Energy Commission — a committee made up of distinguished scientists from outside the government. No single event did more to trigger discussion and reappraisal of national security policy in the United States in the 1950's than the report of the so-called Gaither Committee, a presidential study group drawn from business and other institutions outside the government.[11] Thus, the American system of government "has developed its public service in such a way as to avoid creating a closed bureaucracy." A variety of groups are given an opportunity "to help determine public policy and to assist in its execution through an elaborate system of advisory machinery."[12]

Several factors help to account for the expanding role of outsiders in the internal deliberations of executive agencies. To some extent, it is a product of necessity. In many of the more highly skilled fields, public agencies cannot recruit enough high caliber personnel for full-time employment to meet their needs. The outsider, whether serving as adviser, consultant, or on temporary assignment with the agency, helps fill the gap created by this employment problem. Many talented outsiders will serve executive agencies on a temporary or *ad hoc* basis who could never be attracted to full-time government employment.

Moreover, the role of the outsider is such that he can contribute to the policy-making process certain qualities it would otherwise lack. Having a secure position in an institution other than the agency itself, he can speak his mind without editing his thoughts for fear of reprisal by his administrative superiors in government. This independence of judgment helps promote diversity of opinion within a bureaucratic environment in which the pressures toward

[11] See Morton H. Halperin, "The Gaither Committee and the Policy Process," *World Politics,* Vol. 13 (April, 1961), pp. 360–384. The list of committee members is given on pp. 361–362, footnotes 5 and 6.

[12] Don K. Price, *Government and Science* (New York: New York University Press, 1954), p. 200. See also the discussion of "in-and-outers" in Richard E. Neustadt, "White House and Whitehall," *The Public Interest,* No. 2 (Winter, 1966), pp. 59–61.

conformity may otherwise be very strong. A President or the head of an executive department may also bring in outsiders to protect himself against domination by the strong vested interests and institutional ideologies of the agencies he nominally supervises. In this context, the outsider can play the role of devil's advocate — speaking for points of view that would not ordinarily enter the discussion were it not for his presence. As Fred W. Riggs has noted: "In order for him to control the bureaucratic system, the executive needs a power base outside the bureaucracy itself. Otherwise he becomes a prisoner of his own bureaucracy." [13]

There are, however, certain disadvantages to the outsider's role. From the agency's perspective, there is a measure of irresponsibility in his position, since he does not have to put a policy into effect in an often hostile environment, or live with the consequences of a decision once it has been made. Many advisers may, in addition, have private attachments or interests which color the advice they give the agency. The Dixon-Yates affair, for example, whose tremors shook American politics throughout most of the 1950's, had its origin in the fact that an adviser to the Bureau of the Budget was in a position to benefit personally from the recommendations he made to the government.[14] "Conflict of interest" of this sort remains an enduring problem in the use of outside advisers by executive agencies.

From the outsider's point of view, there are also liabilities attached to his position. While he can give advice, he has no real authority to see that this advice is taken. As an adviser or consultant, the outsider may find that trying to get an agency to follow his suggestions is a good deal like trying to push a box car up hill. It is this consideration which finally leads some outsiders to accept temporary government employment, and agencies like the Policy Planning Staff of the Department of State and the Council of Economic Advisers provide both short-term and full-time employment opportunities through which outside professionals can exert influence at high levels of bureaucratic decision-making.

[13] Fred W. Riggs, "Bureaucrats and Political Development: A Paradoxical View," in Joseph La Palombara (ed.), *Bureaucracy and Political Development* (Princeton: Princeton University Press, 1963), p. 158.

[14] See Aaron Wildavsky, *Dixon-Yates: A Study in Power Politics* (New Haven: Yale University Press, 1962).

An executive agency as well as an individual may find it difficult to exercise real influence when the authority for putting policy decisions into effect rests in other hands. Consequently, an agency that has primarily advisory power may be forced to establish effective liaison with operating agencies in order to prevent its advice from being stillborn. The Council of Economic Advisers, for example, while established primarily to provide the President with competent advice on how best to preserve the health of the domestic economy, has also found it necessary to establish close and continuing relations with a number of executive agencies that wield important powers affecting economic stability. Chief among these agencies are the Bureau of the Budget, the Federal Reserve Board, and the Department of the Treasury. Ultimately, the impact of the Council upon fiscal policy depends upon its ability to exercise influence over these organizations as well as over the President.

The practice of involving outsiders in the internal deliberations of executive agencies is a long-standing tradition in American bureaucracy. Its openness to outside penetration is in fact one of the distinctive characteristics of bureaucracy in the United States. From the point of view of society, this presents the danger of co-optation by the government of individuals who might otherwise be the most informed critics of official policy. Taking a potential critic into camp in this way may thus be regarded as an adroit technique through which the Department of State, for example, can muffle public debate in controversial areas of foreign policy. This is another illustration of Lasswell's "restriction by partial incorporation," [15] buying off potential critics by giving them a place in court.

But the custom of bringing outsiders into government is more than a method by which officials may draw the teeth of their opposition. It is also a means of infusing official policy with the values and attitudes of the community, or at least informed segments of it. More than that, it is an avenue through which the long-term critical capacities of the community may actually be expanded rather than contracted. Sooner or later, many outsiders who are drawn into the policy-making councils of bureaucracy leave government employment. When they do, the inside knowledge they have gained as a result of their government service enables them to become the

---

[15] See Harold Lasswell, *Politics: Who Gets What, When, How* (New York: Whittlesey, 1936), p. 166.

most effective of all critics of official decisions. No one subjected the government's Vietnam policy to more searching or influential criticism than former officials of the Kennedy and Johnson administration.

This is not, of course, to deny the possibility that such bureaucratic migrants may also become apologists for, rather than critics of, official doctrine. Sometimes they may only appear to speak from an independent position as private citizens, since in point of fact they are drawing pay as consultants or advisers from the agency whose policies they are defending. At best, however, the public dialogue as well as the bureaucratic may be greatly improved by having outsiders participate in the internal deliberations of executive agencies. The bureaucratic dialogue may immediately become more spirited, and the public dialogue eventually may become better informed.

CHARACTERISTICS OF THE POLICY SYSTEM

In many ways policy-making within executive agencies is indistinguishable from the process that takes place within legislative assemblies. Agencies respond to group pressures by modifying existing policies or by developing new ones. Bargaining or the adjustment of conflicting interests is as constant a feature of administrative politics as it is of the relations among legislators and legislative committees. Changes in policy tend to be — in Lindblom's phrase — "incremental" in character.[16] Bureaucrats, like legislators, are wary of sweeping innovations which may disturb existing programs.

But while policy-making within bureaucracy bears many similarities to the style of decision-making within legislatures, there are differences also. To some extent these are differences in degree rather than kind, but they are nonetheless far from unimportant — as the discussion which follows will attempt to show. Three characteristics of bureaucratic policy-making are particularly significant

[16] See Charles E. Lindblom, "Policy Analysis," *American Economic Review,* Vol. 48 (June, 1958), pp. 298–312 and "The Science of 'Muddling Through,'" *Public Administration Review,* Vol. XIX (Spring, 1959), pp. 79–88. "Incremental" decision-making is also a central theme in David Braybrooke and Charles E. Lindblom, *A Strategy of Decision* (New York: Free Press of Glencoe, 1963).

in this regard: (1) the fact that authority in executive agencies is hierarchically structured; (2) the strong influence of professional as distinct from political criteria in arriving at decisions; (3) the fact that the policy process is considerably less public in bureaucracy than it is in the legislature.

Hierarchy and Decision-making. One of the most prominent characteristics of bureaucracy as a form of social organization is the distribution of authority in terms of hierarchical rank. In a bureaucratic setting officials at higher echelons normally can exact obedience from their subordinates. Hence, while policy deliberations in the legislature take place among elected officials who are equal in power in the salient respect that they all have but one vote on the questions that come before them, the policy dialogue in bureaucracy takes place among officials who are unequal in rank and consequent authority over final decision.

In recent times there has been a strong tendency in at least the more sophisticated literature of American public administration to discount the importance of hierarchy in bureaucracy. Emphasis has been placed instead on the extent to which subordinate officials can in fact determine policy outcomes — often in defiance of the views held by the heads of their own executive departments. This decentralization of authority has been especially visible in the field of resource administration, where agencies dealing, for example, with water resources have been shown to operate with almost complete autonomy from overhead control.[17]

In the past, this weakness of hierarchy in American administration has commonly been explained in terms of political factors. Subordinate units are able to organize such strong constituency support that their hierarchical superiors are reduced to mere figureheads. Witness, for example, the following description of his own managerial impotence by a former director of the U.S. Employment Service:

> I started as director with a naive idea that I ran it, but I discovered that there was a part of the service that no director ran. This was the Veterans Employment Division, which did

[17] See especially Arthur Maass, *Muddy Waters* (Cambridge: Harvard University Press, 1951).

not even receive its mail in our mailroom. It had a special post office box downtown. When I tried to do something about the division, I learned that it took orders mainly from the Employment Committee of the American Legion. From then on I discussed the work of the division regularly with a committee of the American Legion in Indianapolis.[18]

Another factor that has helped to undermine hierarchical authority in administrative decision-making is the growing power of skilled professions in the work of public bureaucracy. "Especially is the hierarchical procedure weakened," Simon, Smithburg, and Thompson note, "as the social division of labor turns more and more people into indispensable and recondite specialists." [19] Professionalism is rapidly succeeding politics as the principal source of decentralization of authority in American bureaucracy. A subordinate who is master of esoteric skills is no easier to dominate than one backed by a strongly entrenched group of political supporters.

Even in the face of these obstacles, however, hierarchy has become increasingly important in the operations of national bureaucracy in the United States as in other societies. The growing scope and complexity of bureaucratic activities engenders an irresistible need for coordination of effort that can only be achieved by vesting authority over decision-making in the higher ranks of bureaucracy. Left to themselves, subordinate units cannot eliminate duplication of effort or the pursuit of contradictory objectives.[20]

Moreover, the location of decision-making power at higher echelons makes it possible to achieve a more efficient allocation of resources among subordinate units. Certain activities can be centralized to conserve manpower, expenditures can be subject to more rigorous scrutiny by overhead agencies, and priorities can be established to insure that resources are directed toward the more important goals of the organization. Considerations of economy thus

18 Marver Bernstein, *op. cit.,* pp. 94–95.
19 Herbert A. Simon, Donald W. Smithburg and Victor Thompson, *Public Administration* (New York: Alfred A. Knopf, 1950), p. 200. There is a perceptive discussion of the impact of hierarchy upon decision-making in Harold L. Wilensky, *Organizational Intelligence* (New York: Basic Books, 1967), pp. 42–48.
20 *Cf.* also, on this point, the discussion on pp. 33–34.

favor an increase in hierarchical authority, a factor of no small importance in view of the mounting scale of public expenditures.

The doctrine of party government also supports an aggrandizement of hierarchical influence in bureaucracy. A political party that has won an election can only control the reins of government if it can name its own partisans to the commanding heights of bureaucracy where they can oversee and direct the activities of the permanent and professional employees of government. Victor Thompson has written a searching critique of the practice of subordinating skilled specialists to the commands of hierarchical superiors who do not have equal technical competence.[21] However, the objectives of a democratic society often require such subordination. Civilian control of the military, for example, can only be achieved if military professionals are subject to hierarchical control by civilian officials who, while having less knowledge of military matters, are also less insulated from the preferences of the electorate.

The presence of hierarchy as a dominant characteristic of bureaucracy has varied consequences for the policy process. For one thing, it enhances the likelihood that discrete policy decisions will be consistent with each other. Hierarchy is thus an instrument for coherent policy-making, and in this sense at least, an aid to rational calculation in governmental decisions.[22] Activities that cannot be geared together by a more or less self-regulating system of mutual adjustment can be consciously coordinated. Moreover, under a hierarchical system there is much less likelihood that the policy process will be stalemated. The exercise of hierarchical authority can break the log-jams created by conflict between two irreconcilable and equally powerful points of view at lower levels of decision. The growth of hierarchy thus reduces the necessity of relying upon interminable processes of bargaining to arrive at policy decisions.

However, not all the consequences of hierarchy contribute to rational calculation in policy deliberations. The inequality of power inherent in hierarchy means that the views of highly placed individ-

---

[21] Victor A. Thompson, *Modern Organization* (New York: Alfred A. Knopf, 1961).

[22] For an analysis of the advantages of hierarchy as a form of social organization, see Robert A. Dahl and Charles E. Lindblom, *Politics, Economics, and Welfare* (New York: Harper & Bros., 1953), pp. 236–243.

uals carry immense weight, not because of the persuasiveness of their arguments but simply because of the exalted status from which they speak. Subordinates may have to go along with policy decisions reached at higher levels even when they know that their superiors are wrong. Or they may find that their own advice, however well-founded, tends to be discounted because of their low standing in the hierarchy. The rationality of policy under a hierarchical system is thus constantly threatened by the disjunction between power and knowledge.

Ways of dealing with this problem do of course exist, but they are more in the nature of palliatives than antidotes. As noted earlier, subordinates can go over the head of their superior and betray their doubts regarding the wisdom of his judgment to other highly placed officials.[23] This is a course of action not without risk, and it is, therefore, open only to the venturesome. An advisory group made up of individuals having independent status outside the agency can also serve as a check upon folly in high places. But the difficulty here is that, as Dahl and Lindblom point out, men at the top of a hierarchy "decide when, in what conditions, and with whom consultation takes place." [24] Hierarchical superiors, from the President on down, have a penchant for selecting as advisers men who will give them the advice they want to hear.[25]

Hierarchy can thus be an immensely important factor inhibiting discussion and the free exchange of ideas in bureaucratic policy deliberations. In the past, it has been less a problem in American than in other bureaucratic systems. For reasons that are partly cultural and partly structural, bureaucracy in the United States has been characterized traditionally by pluralism rather than hierarchy in organizational design. Whatever disadvantages this system may have had, it presented small possibility that debate might be stifled by deference to the views of a superior. The growth of hierarchy

23 See pp. 92–93.
24 *Op. cit.*, p. 227.
25 This is not, of course, invariably the case. For example, the Gaither Committee, though appointed by President Eisenhower, was severely critical of his administration's defense policies. Moreover, as Halperin points out: "It served as an effective communication procedure to bring before the attention of the President and his principal advisers concerns which were being felt at the middle and upper levels of the operating agencies but which had not filtered through to the White House." *Op. cit.*, p. 384.

thus presents a continuing challenge to develop ways of dealing with the repressive effects it may have upon the policy dialogue.

The Professionalization of Policy. As has been noted earlier, bureaucracy is a governmental habitat in which expertise finds a wealth of opportunities to assert itself and to influence policy. Don K. Price once wrote that "the development of public policy and the methods of its administration owed less in the long run to the processes of conflict among political parties and social or economic pressure groups than to the more objective processes of research and discussion among professional groups." [26] This is the sense in which bureaucracy contributes to the impact of expertise upon policy decisions. It provides a setting in which experts in and out of government can get together to work on policy problems. Sometimes this occurs long before these problems become legislative issues or matters of public debate. In national security policy, for example, controversies over the feasibility of a hydrogen bomb, the need for greater expenditures on civil defense, and the wisdom of constructing an anti-missile system, were issues in bureaucracy long before they became matters of general public concern.

This is not, however, to suggest that political considerations are unimportant in bureaucratic deliberations. Nothing could be further from the truth. As earlier discussion has tried to show, agencies are part of the political system and their activities inevitably reflect the values and interests of outside groups. Certainly an agency's calculations as to the views of its constituency play a major role in the positions it takes on policy questions. It is rare to find an agricultural agency, for example, coming up with policy recommendations that are highly disadvantageous to the groups it serves merely because its own impartial analysis leads it to certain inevitable and irresistible conclusions.[27]

An executive agency, in addition, has certain power interests of its own to take into account in its evaluation of policy questions.

26 *Op. cit.,* p. v.

27 For an interesting account of the troubles that beset one agricultural agency when it pursued research to conclusions that were disadvantageous to a group that considered itself part of the agency's constituency, see Charles M. Hardin, "The Bureau of Agricultural Economics Under Fire: A Study in Valuation Conflicts," *Journal of Farm Economics,* Vol. XXVIII (August, 1946), pp. 635–668.

As the history of the Department of Labor clearly reveals, an administrative organization's fortunes do not necessarily coincide with those of its constituency. During the 1930's, when labor legislation was taking giant steps forward under the impetus of the New Deal, the scope of the Department of Labor's administrative authority at first remained stationary, and then gradually even began to decline. While the department was suffering this setback, the trade union movement, upon which it chiefly depended for political support, was achieving a marked advance in membership and power.

Hence an agency's participation in the policy process is bound to reflect its own distinct power interests quite apart from the needs of its constituency. Questions involving administrative jurisdiction, or the allocation of appropriations among different programs, will inevitably touch an agency's sensibilities about its own organizational stature. No agency can be expected to preside enthusiastically over its own liquidation, and its perspectives on policy are bound to be shaped to some degree at least by considerations of its own organizational self-interest.

It is important, therefore, to guard against the fallacy — so dear to the heart of the American reform tradition — that a policy issue can be de-politicized by turning it over to bureaucracy. It is clear that most policy issues have a zero-sum quality — gains by some groups will have to be offset by losses for others. The decisions of bureaucrats, no less than those of politicians, will involve a redistribution of costs and benefits, and will as an inevitable result be political in nature. Moving authority for decision from politicians to bureaucrats means only that decisions will be made by different people and will result in a different allocation of resources among conflicting groups.

At the same time, however, it is equally vital to avoid the opposite fallacy of assuming that all policy-making in bureaucracy is entirely politicized — that technical and professional considerations have no weight whatsoever except perhaps as window-dressing. The truth of the matter is that a great many policy judgments hinge on technical advice that only professional personnel can supply. The Public Health Service, for example, cannot make policy decisions or recommendations with respect to the smoking of cigarettes as a health problem until it has obtained the best scientific advice available on the relationship between smoking and a variety of illnesses now linked with the use of tobacco.

Likewise, a President, involved in the critical choices he has to make in the area of national security policy, will want to have the best advice he can get — whether from scientific or military sources — on the technical feasibility of certain courses of action. If a President chooses to ignore professional opinion altogether, the political consequences in terms of his own interests can be highly disadvantageous if not disastrous. Consequently, from the point of view of self-preservation alone, politicians are obliged to lean heavily upon the advice of bureaucratic experts in making policy decisions.

The importance of preserving the independence and integrity of certain kinds of expertise in government is thus very great. Traditionally, public agencies performing educational functions, like state universities, or at the national level governmental organizations engaged in a research function, like the Bureau of Labor Statistics or the Bureau of Standards, have been granted — by law or custom — a great deal of administrative autonomy. This freedom has been justified on the practical grounds that the performance of such functions as education and research demands an atmosphere completely free from political pressure.

But as more and more agencies play a policy-making role which requires reliance upon expert or at least non-political standards, the need for professional autonomy begins to assert itself in all phases of bureaucratic policy-making. If policy decisions are to be effective, they have to be informed by honest technical advice. This candor can only be secured if professionals are protected from reprisal for policy findings or recommendations that may be offensive to politically potent groups.

In some cases, an executive agency may choose to isolate a unit within its own organization from outside pressures, or even visibility, and charge it with making recommendations on politically sensitive issues. In this way an agency can at least be certain that non-political criteria are taken into account in making policy decisions, even though political constraints may prevent decisions from being made on the basis of these criteria alone. This was the strategy followed by the Office of Price Administration during World War II, when it set up a Gasoline Eligibility Committee within its own organization to make recommendations to policy-making officials in terms of objective factors on the highly inflammable issue of allocating gasoline among domestic consumers.[28] With such a unit, an agency has some assurance that its policy judgments are not being completely politicized.

In view of the roles which both political and non-political criteria play in the bureaucratic policy process, the framing of public policy in a bureaucratic setting can be seen to involve a constant interplay between two quite different sets of factors. It becomes in effect a mixed system of politics and professionalism. Clearly political considerations have to be taken into account in bureaucratic policy-making in terms of the impact of decisions upon the outside community. At the same time, however, policy decisions certainly cannot "fly in the face" of professional advice when there is agreement among the experts as to the technically sound course of action.

The way in which political and administrative criteria interact in executive agencies can be seen in a decision made in 1948 to close four field offices of the Department of Commerce. The forty-six field offices maintained by the department were first ranked in terms of the number of requests for information they received each month. The Secretary of Commerce then proceeded to select four offices for elimination from the fourteen which ranked lowest on this quantitative scale. While purely administrative criteria had determined which fourteen offices would be considered for elimination, political considerations were prominent in deciding which four out of the fourteen would actually be abolished.[29]

Under the system followed in the Department of Commerce field service case and in similar situations, a decision must not clearly flout professional or non-political criteria. Other considerations can enter the decision-making process only when a decision is defensible on technical grounds. An agency head would leave himself far too vulnerable to criticism if he made decisions that were altogether indefensible in terms of professional standards. At the same time, any objective criteria used would ordinarily leave room for the exercise of discretion. An executive's options are not foreclosed by the findings of his professional staff.

The need for such discretion in the framing of bureaucratic policy is certainly clear. In many areas of policy it is impossible to

28 Harold Stein, *op. cit.*, pp. 749–759.

29 See Kathryn Smul Arnow, "The Department of Commerce Field Service," The Inter-University Case Program (University, Alabama: University of Alabama Press, 1954).

develop quantitative criteria as a basis for decision. Judgments must be made on the basis of incomplete evidence or on the basis of qualitative factors for which there is no evidence whatsoever. To be sure, this sometimes permits decisions to be affected by political considerations of a crude kind. At worst, administrative decisions may even be used to reward friends and punish enemies.

At the same time, however, such discretion also makes possible decisions that take into account a much broader range of considerations than are always encompassed within the perspective of a particular professional group in bureaucracy. Military officials, for example, may not see the diplomatic implications of a course of action they are recommending. Or doctors considering the location of a new city hospital may not give adequate weight to the needs and interests of the prospective patients who will use this medical facility.[30] It is thus possible to see and to find examples of "politics" as corrupting the process of professional decision in bureaucracy. It is also possible to see it as greatly expanding the horizons of bureaucratic decision-makers and enabling policy to satisfy the needs of much wider segments of the public.

Secrecy and Public Policy. The policy process as it is carried on within legislatures is by no means entirely public in character. In the national government, for example, a great many legislative committee meetings at which vital policy decisions are reached are held in secret. The appropriations committees and subcommittees of the House convene in private to determine the level of support to be given each agency and program — the most important perhaps of all policy decisions Congress has to make. The conference committee meetings at which differences between House and Senate bills are hammered out, are also shrouded in secrecy, or, in less invidious terms, conducted in private.[31]

[30] Decisions on the location of facilities such as schools and hospitals often generate such conflicts between professional and community groups. See, for example, Edward Banfield, *Political Influence* (New York: The Free Press of Glencoe, 1961), pp. 15–56, 159–189.

[31] The Congressional Quarterly periodically issues a report on the number of legislative committee sessions conducted in private. See, for example, *Congressional Quarterly Weekly Report*, Vol. XXV (April 21, 1967), pp. 642–644. It should be noted that some of this legislative secrecy results from the fact that executive officials in, for example, the national security area, do not wish to testify at public hearings. Much of it, however, is at the instigation of the legislature itself.

At the same time, however, the legislature is primarily a public institution. The public, if not always the private, activities of its members are open to constant scrutiny from the outside world. Its debates are conducted in public. The investigations and interrogations of its committees, if not visible on a day-to-day basis, are eventually printed in exhaustive detail as a public record. Whatever disadvantages the legislative policy-making process may exhibit, it has a striking asset — the fact that its deliberations and concerns are so easily known to those who will be affected by them.

The bureaucratic policy process is, by way of contrast, a quite invisible part of government. The environment of bureaucracy is a cloistered sanctuary as compared with the limelight of publicity in which a legislative assembly normally operates. Though an executive agency may hold public hearings, or conduct press conferences, or release news bulletins of one kind or another, it controls, to a far greater extent than does the legislature, the information available to the public on its internal deliberations and decisions. The meetings, conferences, negotiations, and agreements through which bureaucratic policy decisions are reached can only be dimly seen through the opaque exterior which an administrative agency presents to the outside world. In some areas of administrative activity information is made available only through "leaks," interviews with "informed" sources, or an unexpected disclosure of secrets that were meant to be kept by a departing member of the inner circle. Bureaucracy did not invent secrecy in American government. The Founding Fathers, for example, found it expedient to conduct the deliberations of the Constitutional Convention at Philadelphia in 1787 in private long before there was an administrative establishment of any consequence in the United States. But the growth of bureaucracy in American government has certainly brought about an enormous expansion in the secretiveness with which public policy is made.[32]

There are important respects in which this secrecy contributes

---

[32] The most careful investigation we have of administrative secrecy in modern American government comes from the hearings conducted during the Eisenhower administration by the Subcommittee on Government Information of the House Committee on Government Operations. The Committee has continued to operate since 1960 but at a somewhat decelerated level of activity. See Robert O. Blanchard, "A Watchdog in Decline," *Columbia Journalism Review*, Vol. V (Summer, 1966), pp. 17–21.

to the effectiveness of governmental decisions. At least in the early stages of policy development, a good many proposals benefit from private discussions. It is possible, for example, to explore certain courses of action in private that could much less easily be discussed in public, such as the use of the American government's funds to disseminate information on birth control at home or abroad. Except for a few hardy individuals, "thinking about the unthinkable" — in Herman Kahn's revealing phrase — is an enterprise much more easily conducted in private than in public.

Since privacy is conducive to candor in policy deliberations, administrative policy-making may permit a more honest exploration of alternatives than is possible in the legislature. Men are less often compelled to edit out of their discussions "dangerous thoughts" that might get them into trouble if they were widely known. Such privacy would be an unqualified benefit to rational calculation in policy deliberations were it not for the fact, previously noted, that it also serves to constrict the number of alternatives considered by excluding many informed individuals from the discussion process.[33]

The greater degree of privacy characteristic of bureaucratic operations may also promote accommodation and compromise in the development of public policy. Participants in administrative discussions can back down more easily on positions they have previously taken if they have not put their earlier point of view on public record. Compromise solutions that may be difficult to explain to constituents can be more easily agreed to in private than in public, since the responsibility for decision is in this case obscure. Compromise is always a mixed blessing from the point of view of the groups whose interests are involved. Since stalemate would be a worse alternative, privacy has a constructive effect upon the policy process by encouraging such mutual adjustment of interests.

Even though there are advantageous aspects of privacy in policy deliberations, the fact remains that the costs of this characteristic of bureaucratic policy-making are also high. Many executive officials make decisions on policy questions without having full access to the facts in possession of the government that are relevant to these decisions because of the restrictions of secrecy. When policies are determined in private, the sources of influence on these decisions

[33] See p. 5.

may be unknown, and many groups whose interests are affected may not be consulted at all.[34]

Finally, it is much more difficult to identify and reverse mistakes when policy deliberations and decisions are made in secret by some chosen few — the saints rather than the sinners. This is a particular problem in foreign affairs where the possibility of irreversible error — of a *fait accompli* that cannot be undone — is heightened by the fact that so much of policy formulation takes place in the cloistered corridors of bureaucracy. In domestic policy, on the other hand, there is such a constant process of interaction among executive agencies, legislative committees, and community groups that very little of what is decided can be long concealed.

The paradoxical fact of the matter is, therefore, that while bureaucracies have been developed to enhance rationality in decision-making, they have certain inherent characteristics, including both a hierarchical distribution of authority and the maintenance of secrecy regarding internal deliberations, that often act as severe handicaps to their ability to arrive at rational decisions. And because of the power large-scale organizations generate, irrational decisions on their part can have awesome consequences. As a result, efforts are constantly being made to improve the rationality of administrative decisions. The chapter that follows discusses some of the steps currently being taken in this direction.

[34] An analysis of the impact of administrative secrecy upon policy decisions may be found in Wilensky, *op. cit.*, esp. pp. 66–74, and Francis E. Rourke, *Secrecy and Publicity: Dilemmas of Democracy* (Baltimore: The Johns Hopkins Press, 1961), pp. 75–86.

CHAPTER SIX

New Designs for
Policy-Making

The central concern of this chapter is with recent attempts to re-style the system through which policy proposals and decisions are made in executive agencies. As administrative agencies have expanded their role in the policy process, there has been a growing effort to increase the effectiveness with which they play this role. This effort has moved in three principal directions. The first is the drive to reorganize the executive branch of government to shift administrative authority to the upper levels of the hierarchy where it is believed that a more inclusive range of interests can be taken into account in reaching decisions. This desire to broaden the perspective of policy-makers is closely linked with the historic quest for the public interest in administrative decision-making.

The second of the new management styles in public administration is the increasing resort to quantitative data and empirical methods of analysis as a basis for policy decisions. The techniques of operations research and systems analysis are coming into increasing vogue in administrative policy-making. Most dramatic has been the apparent success of the Department of Defense in using cost-effectiveness studies in the development of national security policy. This has led to the belief that PPBS (the planning-programming budgeting system) can be applied throughout the government to provide the support of hard data for policy judgments.

Finally, there is an expanding search for administrative arrangements which will encourage vitality and creativity in the bureaucratic policy system. In the past the problem of bureaucracy has often been defined as that of preventing executive agencies from exercising their powers with excessive vigor. Today, however, it is the lack of energy and enthusiasm in bureaucracy that is more frequently the object of complaint. Bureaucracy has become increasingly identified with a lethargic attitude toward innovations in public policy, and reformers have begun to center their attention upon the task of stimulating new life in old organizations.

THE QUEST FOR BROADER PERSPECTIVES

The way in which policy is formulated in executive agencies is commonly subject to the same criticism that is leveled at policy-making within the legislative branch of government. It is asserted that administrative policy decisions tend to reflect too narrow a set of interests. Because authority for designing programs is widely dispersed among subordinate units of the executive branch, policy responds not to the needs of broad segments of the public, but more commonly to the pressures of small clientele groups that hold individual bureaus in captivity.

As a result, it has been a primary objective of administrative reform for at least the past three decades to reshape the structure of the executive branch so that power is centered, not at the lower and presumably more parochial echelons of bureaucracy, but in the hands of departmental executives where it is expected that the interests of wider segments of the public will be taken into account in making policy choices. The location of decision-making power in subordinate agencies and bureaus is thus identified in the reform theory of administrative organization with a limited perspective in policy-making, while the transfer of power to top-level executives has been looked upon as a method by which the horizons of policy can be greatly broadened.

The effort to achieve an executive-centered system of administrative organization has been vigorously pursued at all levels of government in the United States. However, as is usually the case in matters of administration, the national government has taken the lead in organizational reform. The report of the President's Committee on Administrative Management in 1937, as well as the findings and recommendations of two Hoover Commissions in 1949 and 1955, have led the way toward a very substantial expansion in executive authority in national administration in the United States. This administrative reorganization has had a variety of objectives, including the saving of money by eliminating duplication of effort, and the grouping of related activities into cohesive units. But at the heart of the reorganization movement has been the belief that policy-making can be more far-sighted and comprehensive in outlook when responsibility for decision rests with higher rather than lower authority.

The movement toward a more hierarchical system of organization is part of the long-standing quest in the United States for administrative arrangements that will enable and encourage executive agencies to promote the "public interest" in their decision-making processes. To be sure, there has not always been agreement in the literature of public administration on the meaning of so elusive a concept as the public interest. Some have seen it as signifying no more than the sum of the private interests affected by particular administrative decisions, while others regard it as embodying interests that transcend the needs of particular groups in the community. But there would certainly be widespread agreement with the proposition that this public interest standard requires administrative agencies to take the needs of broader as well as narrower publics into account in designing their policies and procedures.[1]

However, even as the reorganization movement has been largely successful in centralizing authority for decision-making in the hands of departmental executives, voices have increasingly been heard suggesting that the old-fashioned system of dispersed authority in administrative organization is not altogether without value in terms of effective policy-making. What might be called a revisionist critique of the reform movement in administrative organization has thus begun to emerge at the very moment when this movement has largely won the day and become in fact the "conventional wisdom" on questions of organizational design.

[1] For a discussion of efforts to use the "public interest" as a touchstone in appraising administrative decision-making, see Pendleton Herring, *Public Administration and the Public Interest* (New York: McGraw-Hill, 1936), esp. pp. 377–399; Emmette S. Redford, *Ideal and Practice in Public Administration* (University, Alabama: University of Alabama Press, 1958), pp. 107–137; Glendon Schubert, *The Public Interest* (New York: Free Press of Glencoe, 1960), esp. pp. 64–74, 106–123, 173–186; and Frank J. Sorauf, "The Public Interest Reconsidered," *Journal of Politics*, Vol. XIX (November, 1957), pp. 616–639.

It is, for example, now being pointed out that a structural pattern under which administrative authority is widely distributed has the advantage of promoting a variety of points of view and a more spirited dialogue among executive agencies in the development of policy. In an analysis of President Franklin D. Roosevelt's style as an administrator, Arthur M. Schlesinger, Jr., argues that the secret of Roosevelt's success was his ability to keep administrative authority scattered to generate disputes among his subordinates which would broaden his own options while preventing any one adviser from gaining excessive influence over him. Roosevelt, writes Schlesinger, "deliberately organized — or disorganized — his system of command to insure that important decisions were passed on to the top. His favorite technique was to keep grants of authority incomplete, jurisdictions uncertain, charters overlapping." [2] It should be noted, however, that if Roosevelt derived such advantages from a system of decentralized administrative authority, he also, as President, did a great deal to further administrative centralization, through, for example, the appointment of the President's Committee on Administrative Management, and the steps he subsequently took to carry out its recommendations.

The fact that dispersion in administrative authority enlivens the process of discussion within bureaucracy is not the only ground on which it can be defended. The argument can also be made that such fragmentation helps to link authority with knowledge, insofar as the professional personnel in subordinate bureaus and agencies commonly know more about the technical aspects of the policy issues with which they are dealing than do departmental executives. From this perspective, recent efforts to shift authority from bureaus up to departments can be looked upon as aggravating the split between knowledge and power that is endemic in modern bureaucracy.[3] Under a system of centralized authority, bureau chiefs inevitably find themselves being overruled by department heads whose professional competence is far less than their own. While these departmental executives may have a broader perspective on

[2] Arthur M. Schlesinger, Jr., *The Coming of the New Deal* (Boston: Houghton Mifflin Co., 1959), pp. 527–528. *Cf.* also on this point the discussion in Richard E. Neustadt, *Presidential Power* (N.Y.: John Wiley & Sons, 1960), pp. 156–158.

[3] The best treatment of this problem is by Victor Thompson, *Modern Organization* (New York: Alfred A. Knopf, 1961).

the problems under consideration, they lack the depth of knowledge on particular issues that their subordinates possess.

Moreover, it is not always certain that officials who are more highly placed in bureaucracy will actually have a clearer view of the public interest in administrative decision-making than their subordinates. Aaron Wildavsky, for one, argues to the contrary:

> . . . the partial-view-of-the-public interest approach is preferable to the total-view-of-the-public interest approach, which is so often urged as being superior. . . . The danger of omitting important values is much greater when participants neglect the values in their immediate care in favor of what seems to them a broader view. . . . A partial adversary system in which the various interests compete for control of policy (under agreed-upon rules) seems more likely to result in reasonable decisions — that is, decisions that take account of the multiplicity of values involved — than one in which the best policy is assumed to be discoverable by a well-intentioned search for the public interest for all by everyone.[4]

Wildavsky's argument here parallels very closely the defense by Charles E. Lindblom of fragmented as opposed to comprehensive approaches to policy development: "different points of view taken by the different groups in government serve to make each group something of a watchdog for certain variables against others."[5]

But while such voices of dissent have been heard with increasing frequency, there has not yet emerged any clear alternative to the hierarchical distribution of authority called for by the prevailing theory of organizational reform in public administration. Official studies and reports at all levels of government still recommend an increase in hierarchy as the standard way of improving the organizational design of the executive branch. Limitations on administrative centralization today largely rest on practical rather than theoretical considerations. Subordinate agencies represent important

[4] Aaron Wildavsky, *The Politics of the Budgetary Process* (Boston: Little, Brown and Co., 1964), pp. 166–167.

[5] Charles E. Lindblom, "Policy Analysis," *American Economic Review,* Vol. 48 (June, 1958), p. 306. More distantly, Wildavsky's viewpoint corresponds to the concept of "piecemeal" social planning developed in the work of Karl Popper, *The Open Society and Its Enemies* (New York: Harper & Row, Torchbook edition, 1963), esp. Vol. I, pp. 157–168.

repositories of specialized skills, and as long as knowledge is widely distributed at lower levels of the hierarchy, power must in large measure follow suit.

In any case, it is not inevitable that a choice be made in designing a policy system between an arrangement which allows for the articulation of specialized and intense interests, and one which reflects the needs of broader and less self-conscious publics. The fact of the matter is that it is possible to incorporate both perspectives in the development of policy in any area. In public higher education in the states, for example, the individual colleges and universities have been left with substantial autonomy to promote their own interests, while at the same time it has become increasingly common to establish a coordinating agency or "super-board" to look at higher education from the perspective of the needs and problems of the entire state. In this way, both Wildavsky's "partial-view-of-the-public interest" and a "total-view-of-the-public interest" may simultaneously inform and guide policy development. Incremental and comprehensive ways of looking at policy issues need not always be mutually exclusive.

DATA AND DECISIONS

No development in public administration in recent years has aroused more widespread interest than the increasing attempt to use quantitative data as a basis for making policy decisions. This trend toward quantification in decision-making partly reflects the fact that management techniques are now available such as operations research and systems analysis which greatly enhance the capacity of administrators to base their decisions upon hard data rather than speculation and hunch. In addition, the vast sums of money now being expended by executive agencies create strong public pressures for greater economy. Since it promises to bring about a more efficient use of financial resources to achieve program goals, quantification thus has great political appeal as well as management utility.

The changing technology of management which has given rise to the new vogue for quantification largely reflects innovations in software, in the sense of techniques such as cost-benefit analysis which make it possible to link data to decision more effectively. But it rests upon changes in management hardware as well, particularly the advent of electronic data-processing equipment. Computers have an extraordinary capacity to sort out large masses of information and to do so with a speed that enables data to be compiled soon enough to have an impact upon decision. To be sure, most of the employment of computers to date in public as in private administration has been in the routine areas of decision — helping administrators keep track of payrolls, clients, and other management records. The use of computers at more complex levels of policy decision is as yet very limited in its development. Eventually, simulation techniques may make it possible to test the impact of high-level decisions on a computer before they are put into effect.[6]

The best publicized development in the use of quantitative methods in policy analysis has been the establishment in the executive branch of PPBS — a planning-programming budgeting system designed to provide executive agencies with a means of clearly identifying and ranking their major goals, and at the same time to supply a more accurate measure of the cost of alternative ways of achieving these objectives. This system was initiated in the Department of Defense in 1961 in an effort to obtain a maximum return on the vast sums of money being expended to achieve national security objectives. In 1965 it was extended by President Johnson to include a wide variety of civilian agencies as well.

Under PPB each executive agency is required to define its goals as carefully as it can, and to measure the value of all programs in terms of their ability to help it achieve its objectives. The expectation is that such an analysis will enable an agency to support its budgetary requests with hard data which show that it will obtain maximum results with the money it expects to receive. PPB has deep roots in the history of the public budgetary process in this country. Earlier innovations in fiscal administration such as performance and program budgeting were also designed to relate the use of resources to the attainment of objectives.[7] What is perhaps

---

[6] Some of the more advanced uses of computers in administrative decision-making are explored in Herbert Simon, *The New Science of Management Decision* (New York: Harper & Row, 1960). See also George P. Shultz and Thomas L. Whisler (eds.), *Management Organization and the Computer* (New York: Free Press of Glencoe, 1960).

[7] The historical antecedents of PPB are traced in Allen Schick, "The Road to PPB," *Public Administration Review*, Vol. XXVI (December, 1966), pp. 243–258. See also the letter by Frederick C. Mosher in the *Public Administration Review*, Vol. XXVII (March, 1967), pp. 67–71.

most new about PPB is the range of sophisticated techniques it uses to measure and compare the costs and benefits of alternative programs, and the primacy it gives to the new management technology in making policy decisions as well as in channeling resources toward the achievement of policy objectives.

There have been many criticisms of the PPB system in and out of government circles. It is, for example, frequently pointed out that the system works with real effectiveness only in areas where administrative objectives can be translated into quantitative terms. For this reason, the Department of Defense was ideally suited for the inauguration of PPB since the achievement of defense goals is so easily tied to the construction and procurement of weapons systems. Alternative ways of assuring the nation's security can thus be expressed in dollar figures and subjected to comparative evaluation on a quantitative basis.

Other programs, however, have proven stubbornly resistant to the magic of managerial science. Unlike defense, foreign policy objectives cannot readily be converted into budgetary alternatives. Cost-benefit ratios are difficult to work out in an area in which the pursuit of program goals is not primarily a matter of spending money.[8] Similar difficulties confront efforts to apply PPB to other non-defense programs. Hard facts on which measures of achievement can be based are hard to come by. Who, for example, can calculate the ultimate benefits that may accrue to society from a federally financed program of educational enrichment designed for slum children in the elementary grades? The task of measuring the costs of a particular course of action can also be extraordinarily difficult, especially when it is necessary to bring non-monetary costs within the sphere of calculation.

Moreover, neither PPB nor any system of quantification now available permits comparisons of the relative pay-off of achieving disparate goals such as welfare, education, or public health. The hard choices of policy, allocating scarce resources among widely different programs, still remain essentially political in character. No set of quantitative techniques can transform policy-making into a purely managerial process. Whether it is more important to use

[8] See in this regard the initial memorandum of the Senate Subcommittee on National Security and International Operations, *Planning-Programming-Budgeting*, 90th Cong., 1st session, committee print, August 11, 1967.

resources to achieve foreign policy objectives, or to spend them on one or more of a variety of domestic programs are questions which defy analysis in cost-benefit terms.

The incommensurability of policy goals thus represents something of a limitation upon the effectiveness of PPB, since it focuses the application of the new system upon sub-optimizing situations, where the goal to be reached is agreed upon, and dispute centers on the question of which of a variety of alternative techniques will best achieve this objective at the lowest cost. The Department of Health, Education, and Welfare, for example, has developed very useful measures of the costs of different public health programs designed to control specific diseases.[9]

At the same time, however, the fact that PPB does have such limitations provides reassurance for those who fear that the new managerial technology will strip power from the public and its elected representatives and shift it to a technocratic elite skilled in operations research, systems analysis, and the use of the new computer hardware. The fact of the matter is that politics plays a central role even in a computerized policy process. As already noted, PPB cannot make policy decisions which involve a choice between conflicting values — the relative importance of, for example, rehabilitating slum areas as opposed to a highway construction program. The larger decisions of public policy thus remain inextricably a matter of public preference.

Moreover, with or without PPB, pressures from community groups, or the calculations of politicians regarding the opinion of these groups, still represent salient factors in making policy choices. While a particular program may rank very low on the scale of cost-benefit ratios, if it enjoys extensive public support, or if the President or a sufficient number of congressmen calculate that it has broad public appeal, then its adverse standing in terms of economic rationality is not likely to be a fatal defect. Now as in the past, policy responds to the balance of forces within the community, or the perceptions of politicians regarding this balance, as well as to the analytical data generated by PPB or any other rationalizing device. Hence, political considerations, in the sense of both value conflicts and the play of conflicting forces within the community,

[9] See Elizabeth B. Drew, "HEW Grapples with PPBS," *The Public Interest*, No. 8 (Summer, 1967), pp. 9–29.

continue to have a major influence upon administrative decisions even in a setting of managerial science.

From the point of view of an executive agency itself, it is often imperative to follow a strategy of organizational opportunism in the pursuit of its goals, no matter what priorities strict adherence to cost-benefit data might seem to require. A program for which a great deal of community support exists at a particular point in time may have to be vigorously pursued even though costs are high and benefits relatively low, in order that the opportunity created by an immediately favorable climate of opinion may not be missed. Adroit administrative statecraft is no less imperative now than it was before the advent of the new managerial science.

At its best, PPB serves as an important instrument of clarification in the design and development of an executive agency's program. While it may not always provide answers in the quest for policy choices, it certainly centers attention on the important questions and provides a framework within which the pursuit of many objectives can be most intelligently carried on. As one observer puts it: "What the new intellectual techniques, such as those used in PPBS, attempt to provide are methods by which those who make the decisions about how the government should direct its efforts can increase their awareness of the conditions and consequences of their choices and can clarify the elements that, explicitly or implicitly, enter into their judgments." [10]

One of the most important roles PPB can play is in directing the attention of administrators to the measurement of organizational performance. For most agencies there is no subject about which it knows less than how well it is doing on the mission on which it is embarked. The prospect of eventually developing better measures of organizational achievement is thus one of the primary reasons for extending PPB as widely as possible throughout the executive branch.

Again, however, political realities must be taken into account. Investigations conducted in 1967 by Congress and the press disclosed that the Subversive Activities Control Board was accomplishing very little in the way of achieving its statutory objective of identifying and deterring subversive activity. However, in spite of

---

[10] Virginia Held, "PPBS Comes to Washington," *The Public Interest*, No. 4 (Summer, 1966), p. 114.

this evidence of its ineffectiveness, the agency continued to command strong support in Congress and elsewhere. As the work of Edelman brings out, an agency can have enormously important symbolic value for its adherents quite apart from its tangible accomplishments.[11] In the case of the Subversive Activities Control Board, the symbol of opposition to communism that it represents far outweighs in the eyes of its supporters a negative showing on the scale of PPB or any other measuring device.

The greatest danger that PPB presents is the possibility that it may arm error with the seeming support of scientifically established fact, in this way giving ill-advised policies greater credence than they would otherwise have. The effective use of PPB thus requires a recognition of its limitations. This is particularly important because the establishment of PPB tends to have a centralizing effect upon the distribution of administrative authority. In the Department of Defense, for example, such techniques have for the first time given the Secretary of Defense real hegemony over national security decisions. While this centralization of authority in Defense reduces the likelihood of error at lower levels of the military hierarchy, it also enhances the possibility that any mistakes that are made will have major if not awesome dimensions. When this occurs, the finely honed rationalizing instruments of managerial science actually become dispensers of irrationality — catastrophe measured out with mathematical precision.[12]

The fact is that quantitative data may have extraordinary weight in decision-making situations in which most of the considerations involved have tangible dimensions. However inadequate such information may be as a measure of the phenomena it is attempting to describe, numerical measurements may still command a great deal of deference simply because they are precise quantities in a sea of uncertainty. To preserve rationality in decision, it is essential, therefore, that the use of data be hedged about with a sense of the limitations as well as the possibilities of such factual information. A balanced perspective of this kind can be most confidently ex-

[11] See Murray Edelman, *The Symbolic Uses of Politics* (Urbana, Illinois: University of Illinois Press, 1964), esp. pp. 44–72.

[12] For some reservations regarding the role of PPB in national security policy-making, see Klaus Knorr, "On the Cost-Effectiveness Approach to Military Research and Development," *Bulletin of the Atomic Scientists*, Vol. XXII (November, 1966), pp. 11–14.

pected when sophistication in the use of quantitative techniques of analysis is widely distributed throughout the government, so that weak arguments in a policy discussion do not gain an unwarranted advantage merely because they are put in the language of managerial science.

INNOVATION IN BUREAUCRACY

Among the many ways in which the American experience with bureaucracy differs from the European, none is more striking than the fact that executive agencies in the United States have so often been looked upon as major instruments of change in social and economic policy, while in Europe bureaucracy has historically been regarded as a chief source of institutional support for the *status quo*. Indeed it is no exaggeration to say that public bureaucracy has been a revolutionary force in American society insofar as it has provided a channel through which submerged groups could assert their power. Farmers in the last century, and more recently trade unionists and the urban poor have looked to bureaucracy for the redress of their grievances against more powerful segments of society, and the services of executive agencies have provided the means by which the welfare and status of these disadvantaged groups have been greatly improved. In Europe, on the other hand, such groups more commonly have identified bureaucracy as part of the political system which must be overcome if significant changes in public policy are to be achieved.

In the 1930's, for example, public bureaucracy was a principal instrument through which the New Deal revolutionized American society. Agencies such as the Securities and Exchange Commission, the Social Security Board, and the National Labor Relations Board quickly became identified as the major institutions through which the power of the mighty was to be put down, and the welfare of the humble exalted. Certainly it was in this light that these agencies were regarded by business groups hostile to the New Deal. From the point of view of American conservatives, bureaucracy was both the symbol and the source of radical change in American society in the 1930's. Fulminations against bureaucratic power dominated conservative rhetoric, while at the same time defense of bureaucracy came to be a conditioned reflex for the American liberal.

By the 1960's, however, new perspectives on the relationship between bureaucracy and change had begun to emerge. Increasingly, the established bureaucracies in welfare, education, foreign affairs, and a variety of other areas came to be looked upon as an obstacle to imaginative and creative thought in their own area of policy responsibility. Reformers interested in taking bold new steps in dealing with the problems of the "permanently poor," or raising the level of aspirations on the part of children in the slum schools, or in achieving some new breakthrough in international relations that would reduce the possibility of nuclear war found that a frequent source of resistance to change in each of these areas was the executive agency chiefly responsible for policy development. Witness, for example, the following description of the role of public bureaucracy in New York City:

> The leaders of the city's bureaucracies are a conservative force in the political contest. The stakes they seek are primarily those that minimize innovation and change. Their drive for autonomy is largely an effort to reduce the influence of the outside "movers and shakers" upon settled routines. . . . The policy and procedural *status quo* of today, or perhaps yesterday's in some matters, is their accepted milieu. . . . In the city's political process the leaders of the organized bureaucracies are an anchor, not a force driving forward.[13]

As a result, bureaucracy today is as frequently a target of criticism from the left in politics as it is from the right. However, while the burden of complaint from conservatives is likely to be the charge that executive agencies are exceeding their authority, liberal groups more frequently complain that agencies are doing far less than their responsibility requires them to do. On one point, however, there is very often a convergence of viewpoint — the belief that bureaucrats are unimaginative, reluctant to accept new ideas, and extraordinarily slow to abandon policies that are clearly unsuccessful. In short, rigidity in outlook on matters of policy is a characteristic

[13] Wallace S. Sayre and Herbert Kaufman, *Governing New York City* (N.Y.: Russell Sage Foundation, 1960), p. 407. Another recent study which points up the obstructive role of bureaucratic organizations in policy development is Gilbert Y. Steiner, *Social Insecurity: The Politics of Welfare* (Chicago, Ill.: Rand McNally & Co., 1966).

increasingly attributed to bureaucracy by critics from all segments of the political spectrum.

Executive agencies are not, of course, without the means of countering, or at least attempting to mitigate, this tendency to become hidebound in their perspectives on public policy. One remedy available is to follow a so-called "lateral entrance" procedure with respect to the recruitment of new personnel. Instead of filling all executive positions by promotion from within the career bureaucracy, talented outsiders can be brought into an agency at high levels of responsibility. Hopefully, these newcomers will bring to its deliberations a fresh approach to policy problems. At the very least they will not have been so thoroughly indoctrinated in the agency's institutional point of view as to be incapable of looking at problems in any but the traditional way. A chief disadvantage of the practice of confining promotion to members of the career staff is commonly believed to be the fact that they have spent their working lives in the service of the agency and their attitudes have been entirely shaped and limited by its norms and experiences.

To be sure, this lateral entrance procedure may entail substantial costs. For one thing, any freshness of viewpoint that an outsider brings to an agency will almost certainly be accompanied by a lack of actual experience in dealing on a day-to-day basis with the problems that are its central concern. Originality may thus have to be purchased at the price of prudence. While a long-time agency administrator may be "in-bred" in his perspective, and have lost his zest for innovation, he may also have a keen eye for pitfalls that should be avoided in launching a new program.

In addition, the practice of allowing outsiders to make a lateral entrance into high-level positions without having served time in the ranks has a negative impact upon the morale of permanent employees who have spent their entire careers in the service of the agency and who see themselves being excluded from the most responsible jobs in the organization. In the long run lateral entrance can thus make it substantially more difficult to attract imaginative and capable personnel to permanent positions within the agency and in this way may actually reinforce mediocrity in the career staff.

An alternative method for invigorating an administrative agency is to provide permanent officials with an opportunity for experiences outside their own agency. This can be accomplished through mid-career training programs which enable such officials to spend a year at a university. However, there are not many organizations which are habituated to accept the value of a sabbatical arrangement and from which an employee can take leave without damaging his own career prospects. Lateral entrance by outsiders into an agency thus remains a more viable method of introducing new perspectives than temporary service by agency personnel in an environment in which their own outlook may be broadened.[14]

The quickest and most thorough-going method of insuring a fresh approach in administration is to establish a new agency. When it is feasible, this alternative is much preferred by reformers, since it allows for the recruitment of an entirely new cadre of personnel, thus eliminating the necessity of converting old hands to new ideas. A new agency is also free from some of the constraints that limit the flexibility of established organizations, such as a long-standing association with certain pressure groups, or an arrangement of mutual accommodation with legislators upon whom an agency may depend for fiscal support. Moreover, such an agency has not yet acquired the administrative habits and experience that it may eventually come to regard as the sum total of human wisdom in its own area of policy.

Similar in its effect to the creation of a new agency is a significant change in the jurisdiction or resources vested in an existing administrative organization. In the 1960's, for example, a flood of educational legislation greatly broadened the responsibilities of the U.S. Office of Education. This led to an influx of new personnel as well as to a reorganization of the agency which altered not only its internal structure of power, but also the pattern of external influences to which the agency was subject from outside groups.[15] While not all observers would agree that such measures achieved a genuine improvement in the character of the Office of Education, this case does point up the possibility of administrative renaissance — an old agency may be given a new lease on life through administra-

14 Of course, to the extent that an agency practices rotation in assignment, it broadens the perspectives of its career staff. Rotation in assignment does not, however, free an employee from the influence of his own organization.

15 See Stephen K. Bailey, "The Office of Education and the Education Act of 1965," Inter-University Case Program, No. 100. (Indianapolis: Bobbs Merrill Co., 1966).

tive reorganization, the influx of new personnel, or a dramatic shift in the scope of its activities.

Innovation in the development of policy can also be encouraged by the practice of having executive agencies contract with organizations outside of government to undertake studies and make proposals on policy issues. Recent years have seen a proliferation of arrangements at all levels of government under which private organizations perform research at the request of public agencies for the guidance of policy-makers. Much of this kind of activity has been delegated to universities, but a new phenomenon has also emerged — the so-called "side-car" corporation, private organizations like RAND or the Institute for Defense Analyses which exist almost entirely on the revenue they receive from conducting studies for government agencies.

A number of advantages accrue from the use of outside organizations for research purposes. For one thing these organizations are free from the restrictions which surround government hiring procedures and can, as a result, often recruit a very high caliber of professional personnel. Since they have no vested interests to protect in arguing for one line of policy rather than another, the conclusions they arrive at are often regarded as a good deal more reliable than the findings of a research unit under the jurisdiction of a line agency. Within government itself, research is often used not so much to find answers to questions as to build support for solutions that policy-makers have already decided upon, or to advance the jurisdictional interests of a particular agency. Policy studies conducted by outside organizations are not immune to this tendency,[16] but they are less susceptible to it.

Outside organizations can be used not only for advisory or consultative purposes but also for the direct operation of governmentally supported activities. The atomic energy program, for example, as well as a wide variety of research and development projects sponsored by agencies like the National Institutes of Health and the National Aeronautics and Space Agency, are largely carried on

---

[16] See particularly the study of the RAND Corporation by Philip Green, "Science, Government and the Case of RAND: A Singular Pluralism," *World Politics,* Vol. XX (Jan., 1968), pp. 301–326. Green argues that the findings of studies conducted by RAND are largely pre-structured by their governmental sponsors.

through government contracts with outside organizations, particularly, though not exclusively, universities. The Office of Economic Opportunity has administered the overwhelming majority of its antipoverty activities through private, non-profit corporations. This system of what Don K. Price has called "federalism by contract" [17] is to a large extent motivated by the belief that nongovernmental organizations can be considerably more imaginative in their approach to policy problems and much more flexible in their day-to-day operations than public agencies.

[17] Don K. Price, *Government and Science* (New York: New York University Press, 1954), pp. 65–94.

CHAPTER SEVEN

Bureaucracy as a Power Elite

A specter that has haunted American politics throughout this century is the possibility that bureaucrats will come to occupy so commanding a position in the policy process as to become in effect a power elite — dominating all governmental decisions in which they participate.[1] A growing reliance upon the skills of bureaucrats in the operation of modern government has thus been coupled with a pervasive distrust of bureaucratic power. On the part of conservatives this has been largely a fear of civilian bureaucrats taking over areas of social and economic decision that properly ought to be left in private hands. From the liberal side, concern has been centered on the growing power of the national security bureaucracy — not only the military establishment but also such organizations as the Central Intelligence Agency and the Federal Bureau of Investigation.

This fear has often taken extravagant form, exaggerating beyond all bounds of possibility the capacity or likely intention of particular agencies to assume a controlling voice over governmental decisions. Paradoxically, this fear of bureaucracy often co-exists with another attitude with which it is in sharp contradiction — the feeling noted in the previous chapter that bureaucrats are timid, unimaginative, and reluctant to make decisions. The stereotype of a bureaucracy that is boundless in its appetite for power may thus sit in comfortable conspiracy with an image of bureaucracy para-

---

[1] For an analysis of the literature bearing on this problem, see Dwight Waldo, *The Administrative State* (New York: The Ronald Press, 1948), pp. 89–103.

lyzed with indecision when confronted with an opportunity to exercise authority.

In any case, even if bureaucrats had the inordinate desire for power commonly attributed to them, their role in the governmental process is hedged about by a wide variety of constraints which limit their ability to exercise influence. These limitations arise partly from sources external to executive agencies, since bureaucrats do not rule alone in any area of public policy. They rest also upon factors indigenous to bureaucracy itself — "inner-checks" built into the structure of administrative organization and the behavior of bureaucrats.

However, if bureaucrats do not have a monopoly power over policy-making, it is clear that they play a strategic role in the process by which decisions are made. While they are unable to rule alone, no one can rule without them. And when administrators cannot achieve their own goals, they may be able to prevent others from achieving goals to which they are opposed. It is as a "veto group," or perhaps through its ability to keep certain matters from coming to decision at all, that an executive agency may actually exercise its most formidable influence. This chapter examines both the pattern of constraints to which bureaucratic power is subject, and the extent to which executive agencies yet manage to retain a compelling voice in the determination of public policy.

CONSTRAINTS ON BUREAUCRATIC POWER

A fundamental restriction under which bureaucrats operate is the fact that they share control over decisions with other elites in the political system. Whatever else it may be, theirs is not an exclusive power. As important as any of the groups with which they compete for influence are the political elites in both the executive and legislative branches of government. In addition, the leaders of non-governmental organizations with a continuing interest in the issues over which executive agencies have jurisdiction often play as vital a role in the development of policy as public officials — whether elective or appointive. Less pervasive but nonetheless critical is the periodic participation by the courts in the processes of policy-making. The judicial elite has long helped to define and set boundaries upon the power of bureaucrats.

The interaction of bureaucrats with each of these elite groups in the development of public policy will be examined in the section that follows. It should, however, be noted at the outset that bureaucratic influence is by no means a constant factor in the policy process. As pointed out earlier,[2] the bureaucrat may exert measurably more influence in one policy setting than he does in another, or the influence of a particular professional group may be much greater in one governmental jurisdiction than it is in an adjacent community. Significant variations in the balance of power between bureaucrats and other elites may also occur at different periods of time as a result of changes in the external environment in which an agency operates. During a period of international crisis, for example, the influence of the military bureaucracy may rise dramatically, and then recede as the sense of emergency begins to evaporate. "Power in America," David Riesman writes, is "situational and mercurial." [3] Clearly, this is no less true of bureaucratic than it is of other forms of influence.

Competition of Elites. The relationship between bureaucratic and political elites in the United States is enormously complicated by the fact that varied sets of political leaders simultaneously occupy positions of authority with respect to administrative agencies. On the one hand, there is a set of executive politicians with which agencies must share power — a chief executive such as the President, a governor, or a mayor, and his appointed or elected administrative subordinates. On the legislative side, there are, under a bicameral system of representation, two or more groups of leaders who participate with bureaucrats in policy decisions.

In general the presence of these varied political elites in the policy process helps to create a system of multiple constraints upon bureaucratic behavior and decision. Executive agencies in the national government operate within limits set by the President with respect to budgets, personnel, and policy, as well as restrictions imposed by Congress through statutes, appropriation acts, or the threat of investigation. In addition, agencies are subject to patterns of informal political pressure from both legislative and executive

[2] See pp. 57–61.
[3] David Riesman, *The Lonely Crowd* (New Haven: Yale University Press, 1950), p. 252.

leaders because they are so heavily dependent upon these officials for the resources necessary to sustain their programs.

Of course, by winning favor with one political elite, bureaucrats can limit the authority of another. Through the assiduous cultivation of support from key legislative groups, administrative agencies have been able to reduce, sometimes to the vanishing point, the controls exerted over them by executive politicians. An agency can also use one group of legislators as a shield against another.[4] Political elites compete with each other as well as with bureaucrats, and executive agencies often serve as valuable allies in the struggle for power among politicians. However, it is questionable if bureaucrats always increase their influence in the policy system by playing one political elite off against another. When, for example, they decrease the control exercised over them by executive politicians, they may intensify the degree of their subordination to legislative elites to become in effect "legislative agencies." A much more promising strategy is that of building up outside sources of power to which political leaders in both the executive and legislative branches of government will defer.

Traditionally, it has been assumed that bureaucrats derive substantial advantage in their interaction with political elites from both their greater expertise in the technical areas of policy and their continuity in office. However, the fact of the matter is that these assets of expertise and continuity are not always the exclusive possession of the bureaucrat in the American political system. Legislative leaders in key committees may gain as expert a command of policy problems as any of the bureaucrats with whom they deal. In the United States, legislators tend to specialize in their policy interests — a tendency which is encouraged by the strong power vested in legislative committees. This specialization, along with the fact that many legislators enjoy long tenure in office, helps to offset the superior professional qualifications which bureaucrats ordinarily bring to policy deliberations.[5]

In short, it is, as noted before, incorrect to regard a political

---

[4] See J. Leiper Freeman, *The Political Process: Executive Bureau — Legislative Committee Relations* (New York: Random House, rev. ed., 1965), pp. 80–81.

[5] In this connection, see the account of the career of Representative Carl Vinson of Georgia in David B. Truman, *The Governmental Process* (New York: Alfred A. Knopf, 1951), p. 424.

elite's influence as resting solely upon the power of numbers — upon the ability of the population to reflect and generate public pressures, while bureaucratic influence is traced entirely to the professional skills of administrators. Politicians, too, may in time acquire formidable credentials as experts, if they do not bring such credentials with them when they come to office. But if political officials share in the bureaucratic asset of expertise, bureaucrats themselves are not wholly without the ability to mobilize public support in behalf of their own policy positions. The competition between bureaucratic and political elites is thus one in which either side can bring to bear both political and professional resources.

The leaders of non-governmental organizations also represent an elite with which bureaucrats must share power, and thus act as something of a constraint upon bureaucratic influence in the policy process. This is obvious in the case of non-governmental organizations which have an adversary relationship with an executive agency. If a government agency administers laws which limit the discretion of, for example, business organizations, these outside organizations will in turn bend every effort to see to it that the powers of such a regulatory agency are confined within narrow limits.

What is not perhaps quite so obvious is the fact that the leaders of non-government organizations which are allies rather than antagonists of an executive agency may also represent a significant constraint upon the scope of its influence. But in international politics alliances often limit the options open to states which participate in such arrangements — preventing them from following certain courses of action and requiring them to fulfill commitments which they might well prefer to forget. In a similar fashion, the alliances forged by the Departments of Agriculture, Commerce, and Labor with their farm, business, and trade union clientele, while of great value in enhancing the constituency strength of these agencies, nonetheless require that each department defer to the views of its non-governmental allies in adopting policy positions. The development of political support through the negotiation of alliances with outside organizations is thus a means by which the power of executive agencies is circumscribed as well as extended.

In most instances, the non-governmental elites to whose influence an executive agency is susceptible consist of the leaders of groups with specialized occupational, economic, or ideological interests in the area of an agency's policy responsibilities — the family of organizations commonly known as "pressure groups." However, in some areas of policy, it is representatives of the media of communication who generate the most substantial outside constraint upon the decisions and activities of government officials. This fourth branch of government, as Douglass Cater calls it,[6] has a powerful voice in the development of policy because it both reflects and has the power to shape the contours of public opinion. Nowhere is the influence of the media more keenly felt than in the agencies dealing with foreign policy, since only the media have the capacity to gather and disseminate information which may challenge the viewpoint of government officials on areas remote from the average citizen's power of observation.

To be sure, it is always possible for an executive agency to "capture" outside groups or representatives of the media, and to make them in effect either "front organizations" or purveyors of the agency's point of view. As noted earlier, it is a major strategic objective of executive agencies to use outside groups in precisely this way. The leaders of interest organizations can be given quasi-official status as members of an agency's structure of advisory groups — in this way involving them to such an extent in the development of policy that they must inevitably become its defenders rather than its critics. Newsmen, on the other hand, can be given preferential treatment in access to official sources, provided with advance information on pending developments, or given through "leaks" inside information not available to unfriendly journalists. In these and other ways some representatives of the news industry may be corrupted into a relationship of faithful adherence to official policy doctrines.

But in the end the best an executive agency can hope for is partial, not total, control of the network of outside organizations to which its activities are salient. The views of interest organizations are often so various that it is not possible for an agency to develop lines of policy which will satisfy all of them simultaneously. The Department of Agriculture, for example, deals with a host of farm

---

[6] Douglass Cater, *The Fourth Branch of Government* (Boston: Houghton Mifflin, 1959).

organizations that have competitive as well as complementary goals. Even if the leader of an interest organization can be taken into camp by an executive agency, there is no guarantee that he will be able to deliver his followers. Indeed, a trade union leader who hews too closely to the views of executive officials on wage issues may suddenly find himself a leader emeritus. As a matter of fact, there are a great many executive agencies which have all they can do to escape becoming captive to the outside organizations with which they deal. The balance of power situation in which they are involved entirely favors the outside group.

As far as newsmen are concerned, they are — at least in the United States — strongly resistant to a captive role in their relations with executive agencies. For one thing, American journalists have a status of parity with government officials that newsmen abroad seldom enjoy. This high standing gives newsmen in this country a professional pride that insures a measure of independence in their dealings with the government. Moreover, in accordance with the "muckraking" tradition, the American reporter ordinarily conceives of his appropriate role as that of exposing the misdeeds of public officials, and this role perception is itself a strong inhibition against subservience to the government.

Finally, newsmen as a group commonly cultivate an attitude of cynical disbelief toward statements and activities at "city hall" — a term embracing executive agencies at all levels of government. This attitude creates a built-in "credibility gap" of substantial dimensions between newsmen and government officials, and strongly reinforces the independence of reporters. True, reporters are sometimes manipulated by executive agencies into disseminating policy viewpoints that the agency wants the public to accept. At the same time, however, there is no more effective instrument than the news media for ferreting out information that agencies are trying to conceal because it contradicts the tenets of official policy.[7]

In addition to the limitation imposed on their power by political elites and the leaders of non-governmental organizations, bureau-

[7] Analyses of the many-sided relationship between executive agencies and the press may be found in Cater, *op. cit.*, Bernard Cohen, *The Press and Foreign Policy* (Princeton, N.J.: Princeton University Press, 1963), Dan Nimmo, *Newsgathering in Washington* (New York: Atherton Press, 1964), James Reston, *The Artillery of the Press* (New York: Harper & Row, 1967), and William L. Rivers, *The Opinionmakers* (Boston: Beacon Press, 1965).

crats are also subject to restraint from the judicial branch of government. In many areas of policy, the decision of executive agencies can be appealed to the courts. The possibility of such appeal is the greatest with respect to regulatory agencies, since their decisions may have so negative an effect upon the constitutionally protected rights of individual citizens to life, liberty, and property. An agency like the Department of State, on the other hand, may — except for passport cases — seldom have occasion to find itself in court. But the possibility of being haled before a judge and having their decisions overruled represents some kind of check upon all executive agencies.

To be sure, there is a vast area of administrative action which is, in legal parlance, non-reviewable. Partly this is attributable to legal considerations, such as the fact that much of administrative policy-making does not generate cases or controversies which can be taken to court. Partly, however, it rests upon considerations of prudence. When an agency has a continuing relationship of supervision with respect to a private organization or individual, this relationship often breeds acquiescence even to agency actions that are regarded as challengeable in court, since the agency's capacity for reprisal deters assaults upon its authority.[8]

In any event, the outlook is not altogether promising for individuals who choose to contest agency actions in court. From a study of U.S. Supreme Court decisions with respect to ten executive agencies over the decade 1947–1956, Joseph Tanenhaus concluded that "the Court and its individual members favor federal agencies more frequently than they oppose them to a statistically significant degree."[9] Since the 1930's the courts have increasingly tended to give agencies greater latitude with respect to matters vested within their jurisdiction.

Hence, while the possibility of judicial review is a check upon administrative action, it is not an altogether stringent one in the United States. On balance, it is more important in state and local

[8] See also the discussion on this point on p. 54. For a wide-ranging discussion of the ability of executive agencies to exercise power out-reaching their legal authority, see Kenneth C. Davis, *Administrative Law* (St. Paul: West Publishing Co., 1951).

[9] See Joseph Tanenhaus, "Supreme Court Attitudes toward Federal Administrative Agencies," *The Journal of Politics*, Vol. 22 (August, 1960), p. 513. Out of 243 decisions involving the agencies, 168 were favorable to them.

than it is in national administration, since judges at these lower echelons have tended to construe the powers of government more narrowly than jurists in the federal court system. At all levels of government, however, one of the most important effects of judicial review of administrative decisions is to enlarge the role and influence of lawyers in the policy-making process within bureaucracy. Since advice on the legality of proposed courses of action is their specialty, lawyers are in a position to discourage certain policy measures they consider undesirable by declaring that these policies are certain to invoke judicial veto.[10]

The structure of influence over decision-making within executive agencies is thus affected by the fact that bureaucrats share power in the policy process with outside elites. Moreover, lawyers are not the only group inside bureaucracy who benefit from the necessity of negotiating with external forces. The role of budget officers in policy decisions is buttressed by the fact that they play a primary role in the bargaining with political elites which is necessary to obtain fiscal resources. The influence of legislative liaison officials in an executive agency is derived in no small measure from their close association with the legislators whose good-will is vital to the agency's development and even survival. And public information officers can use their intimate contacts with the news media to expand their own influence in policy deliberations within bureaucracy. The participation of outside elites in the policy process thus has a major effect not only upon the nature of the decisions made within bureaucracy, but also upon the identity of those who make them.

The Inner Check. Limitations upon the power of bureaucrats spring not only from the competitive pressures of non-bureaucratic elites but also from factors inherent in bureaucracy itself. Not least important in this respect is the struggle for primacy that is a constant characteristic of the relations among executive agencies. While the overt objective of this struggle is to strengthen the agencies that participate in it, an unanticipated consequence of such inter-

---

[10] For an informative account of the role of lawyers in bureaucratic policy-making, see Victor A. Thompson, *The Regulatory Process in OPA Rationing* (New York: Columbia University Press, 1950), esp. pp. 207–220.

bureaucratic combat is that the agencies involved become much more susceptible to outside control.

In the United States, for example, the various branches of the armed forces have long engaged in vigorous competition for financial support as well as jurisdiction over various weapons systems and combat missions. Somewhat unexpectedly, this competition has played an important role in facilitating civilian control over the military, primarily because it has forced each branch of the service into searching criticism of the defense policies advocated by the others, thus preventing the emergence of a monolithic military point of view on national security matters and enabling outside groups to make their own influence felt by siding with one military organization or another.

Indeed, military units sometimes seem to curry support for their organizational interests by adopting points of view likely to win favor from outside groups, as for example when the Air Force aligned itself with civilian opponents of a universal military training system in advocating a reliance upon air power as an alternative to UMT. As Huntington notes, American Presidents have never had difficulty in finding support among military organizations for whatever defense policies the Chief Executives wished to adopt.[11]

On one occasion, an American President was even able to use the views of a foreign bureaucracy as a counter-weight to the recommendations of his own military establishment. Early in World War II, President Franklin D. Roosevelt came under strong pressure from the American Armed Forces to authorize the establishment of a second front in Europe. He was aided substantially in his resistance to this pressure by simultaneous opposition to such a venture from the British military organizations with which the American high command was then in close consultation.[12]

In recent years, the system of internal checks as a method of controlling the military bureaucracy in the United States has no longer been structured around inter-service rivalry. With the amalgamation of the separate services into a single military establishment

11 See Samuel P. Huntington, *The Common Defense* (New York: Columbia University Press, 1961), pp. 371–372, 113–115.

12 See, in this regard, William R. Emerson, "F.D.R." in Ernest R. May (ed.), *The Ultimate Decision: The President as Commander in Chief* (New York: George Braziller, 1960), pp. 135–177.

under the aggressive leadership of Secretary of Defense Robert S. McNamara, the balance of power has rested instead upon the ability of skilled fiscal technicians in the Secretary's office to offset the influence of military professionals in the framing of defense policy. Throughout the government such fiscal technicians, either old-style budget officers or new-style systems analysts, do in fact play a dominant role in containing the power of professional groups with a commitment to specific policy goals. Competition as a restraint upon bureaucratic power thus operates within executive agencies as well as among them, in the form of a struggle for power among groups playing different roles in the operation of a single agency.

Perhaps the truest kind of "inner check" upon bureaucratic power is not inter-agency rivalry, which requires, after all, a vigorously competitive relationship between two or more executive organizations, but restraints which operate within the personalities of bureaucrats themselves — preventing them from unlawful or excessive use of the power placed in their keeping. Such internalized restraints have as their great advantage the fact that, when they are effective, they operate as a constant presence — exercising a restraining influence in areas of decision known perhaps only to the bureaucrat himself.

Ideally, the bureaucrat's conception of his own role in the governing process can be structured to constitute by itself a substantial check upon the extravagant use of his power.[13] If bureaucrats themselves feel it is necessary to defer to the preferences of citizens in framing public policy, or regard it as reprehensible to use power in ways that infringe upon the liberties of individuals subject to their jurisdiction, then the problem of controlling bureaucratic power is very largely solved at the source. Inhibitions on the part of the bureaucrat may in this case serve as an effective substitute for external controls.

Certainly it is true that in a country like the United States, bureaucrats are, like all other citizens, subject to processes of education as children, and of continuing indoctrination as adults, that stress the importance of adherence to fair play in the relations

[13] The term role is here used in the sense of forms of behaviors expected of, or considered suitable for, individuals occupying a certain position or performing a particular function in an organization. See Abraham Zaleznik, "Interpersonal Relations in Organizations," in James March (ed.), *Handbook of Organizations* (Chicago: Rand McNally and Co., 1965), pp. 589–590.

between government and the citizen, as well as the obligation of public officials to defer to the will of the people. And if bureaucrats were to forget the fact that their proper role is that of the public's servant and not its master, a variety of institutions — including legislative bodies, the courts, and the press — would be quick to remind them of the subordinate nature of their role.

Significant in this respect is the fact that codes of ethics adopted by administrative groups such as city managers characteristically accept a subordinate role for bureaucrats in the governmental process. To be sure this acceptance may be mere lip service, designed to disguise the extent to which bureaucrats actually control policy decisions. At the same time, however, it seems fair to assume that there will be some strain toward consistency on the part of administrative officials, and that a bureaucrat's conception of his role as a limited one will have a restraining effect upon his behavior in office.

There has been a long-standing dispute in the literature of public administration as to whether the more effective way of containing the expansion of bureaucratic power is through the internal restraints just discussed or through the competition among elites outlined in the earlier sections of this chapter. As previously noted, the argument for the primacy of the inner checks rests essentially on the grounds that these controls operate more pervasively and effectively than the efforts at surveillance of bureaucratic behavior by external elites. Given the complexity of modern government, it is, as Carl J. Friedrich has noted,[14] impossible to avoid leaving large amounts of power in the hands of bureaucrats to be used at their discretion.

However, the chief disadvantage of these purely psychological inner checks is that they rely essentially upon the inculcation of virtue, operating through either conscientious scruples on the part of the individual official, or a code of honor or ethics prevailing among an administrative group to which a bureaucrat feels he must conform. But as Herman Finer has pointed out, "reliance on an official's conscience may be reliance on an official's accomplice," since "the political and administrative history of all ages . . . has

14 Carl J. Friedrich, "Public Policy and the Nature of Administrative Responsibility," from Carl J. Friedrich and Edward S. Mason (eds.), *Public Policy* (Cambridge: Harvard University Press, 1940), pp. 3–24.

demonstrated without the shadow of a doubt that sooner or later there is an abuse of power when external punitive controls are lacking." [15]

The competition among elites, on the other hand, rests upon the solid bedrock of human selfishness — the ambition of political and bureaucratic elites alike to pursue and protect their own power interests. It was just such motives as these that the authors of *The Federalist Papers* saw as the most dependable base on which restraints on power could be built realistically into the American constitutional system: "Ambition must be made to counteract ambition. The interest of the man must be connected with the constitutional rights of the place . . . the constant aim is to divide and arrange the several offices in such a manner as that each may be a check on the other — that the private interest of every individual may be a sentinel over the public rights." [16]

THE ENDURING PROBLEM OF BUREAUCRACY

Extensive as the controls over bureaucracy may seem to be, both from external and internal sources, the power of executive officials yet remains an object of intense concern in modern politics. To some extent this anxiety merely reflects the persistent strength of a political mythology in many countries which credits bureaucracy with a good deal more power than it actually has. At the same time, however, it also rests upon well-grounded apprehensions regarding the role of bureaucracy which no system of controls presently in practice can altogether dispel.

For one thing, such controls cannot erase the fact that a decisive power of initiative has now been placed in the hands of executive officials. There is, for example, always the nightmarish possibility that military organizations may use their power over the disposition and use of weapons to precipitate a thermonuclear war that would destroy modern civilization. Against such a holocaust, the controls already discussed in this chapter may seem pitifully inadequate, even though the outbreak of war today is as likely to stem from

[15] Herman Finer, "Administrative Responsibility in Democratic Government," *Public Administration Review*, Vol. I (Summer, 1941), pp. 336–337.
[16] See Roy P. Fairfield (ed.), *The Federalist Papers* (Garden City, N.Y.: Doubleday Anchor edition, 1961), p. 160.

the miscalculations of politicians, or the passions of the public, as it is from precipitous actions on the part of bureaucrats.

Dissatisfaction with the adequacy of controls over bureaucracy in the contemporary world also springs from the fact that these controls are far more effective as checks than they are as spurs to action. Increasingly in the modern state, a primary problem of bureaucracy is seen to be that of administrative inertia — the failure of bureaucrats to deal vigorously and imaginatively with problems that are high on the agenda of public concern. In part this is simply a matter of bureaucrats choosing to ignore problems that lie within their official responsibility, since executive agencies have an enormous capacity for "nondecision." [17] They can see to it that issues do not arise in areas in which, to an outside observer, action may seem to be urgently needed. In part also, bureaucratic inertia manifests itself through the fact that executive agencies find difficulty in shifting their sights when past policies are no longer appropriate to present conditions.

This latter aspect of bureaucratic inertia — the difficulty administrative officials have in admitting and reversing mistakes — sharply contradicts one of the major justifications traditionally offered for transferring power over policy development from legislative assemblies to executive agencies. This was the expectation that administrative agencies would be considerably more flexible than legislatures in their response to changing environmental conditions — mainly because they were organizations continuously in existence, which could use the discretionary authority given them to adapt policy to emerging needs. In point of fact, however, public bureaucracies on frequent occasion have proved to be quite rigid in their policy commitments, unable to change courses of action with which they as institutions or the reputations of their leaders have become identified.

Sometimes the resistance of bureaucracy to new outlooks may be simply a function of the slowness of movement of large organizations — the fact that a broad and complex pattern of consensus must

17 This is a term introduced and used extensively in the analysis of political power in urban communities by Peter Bachrach and Morton S. Baratz, "Two Faces of Power," *American Political Science Review*, Vol. 56 (December, 1962), pp. 947–952, and "Decisions and Nondecisions: An Analytical Framework," *American Political Science Review*, Vol. 57 (September, 1963), pp. 632–642.

be developed before change can take place in vast organizational systems in which there are many centers of power and innumerable points at which decision can be blocked. However, it is also possible for organizations to acquire vested interests in policies that are, from the point of society at large, dysfunctional, and to resist change, not because it is difficult for them to move in response to new stimuli, but simply because they have acquired a stake in the policies they are already following. If existing programs serve the comfort and convenience of a public agency's employees, or conform to their own professional view of what should be done, then they may develop deeply entrenched resistance to any alteration in such policies.

Private organizations can, of course, exhibit this same tendency toward organizational inertia. However, by so doing, they run the risk that the public will cease to purchase, or otherwise support, the goods and services they supply, and a private organization's survival may be quickly threatened by its failure to adapt to the community's needs. Public agencies, on the other hand, perform vital functions that a community cannot do without, and they frequently hold a monopoly position in providing such services. Except in the case of agencies that enjoy only precarious political support, a citizen cannot directly threaten the existence of a public agency as a means of forcing it to put his needs before those it may choose to set for itself.[18]

Moreover, even in situations in which public agencies do not wield such monopoly power, and are linked instead in a policy system with other bureaucratic or non-bureaucratic elites, it is always possible that relations among these groups will more closely resemble oligopoly than they do competition. This is to say that these separate elites may be able to find common interests in the development of policies which will satisfy all their distinct interests simultaneously. The military-industrial complex in the United States, for example, is often identified as just such an arrangement under which military bureaucracies, defense contractors in private industry, and political elites, such as congressmen concerned with military affairs, are linked together in the support of a high level

---

[18] For a systematic analysis of factors affecting innovation in public and private organizations, see James G. March and Herbert A. Simon, *Organizations* (New York: John Wiley & Sons, 1958), pp. 172–210.

of defense spending from which each group derives substantial benefits. In a situation of this sort, the belief that outside elites will serve as effective instruments of restraint upon a government agency may be an illusory expectation.

Discontent with bureaucracy in the modern state also centers on a feature of bureaucratic policy-making already subject to extensive discussion.[19] This is the hierarchical characteristic of executive agencies — the fact that superior officials have considerable power over the careers and hence the views of their subordinates. In this context, it is impossible to expect anything resembling a completely free discussion in which all alternatives are given equal consideration. Especially when they are involved in conflict situations with external groups, organizations will inevitably tend to emphasize solidarity rather than dissent as an institutional virtue. A decision-making system subject to constraints of this sort is incapable of meeting all the requirements of a democratic society committed — in theory at least — to full and frank exploration of all options as a prerequisite to rational decision.

Limitations such as these which seem to be inherent characteristics of large organizations have led to a search for remedies for the problems posed by bureaucracy more radical than any of the techniques of control discussed in the earlier sections of this chapter. The most drastic of all cures available for the ills of bureaucracy is simply that of attempting to solve as few social problems as possible through the creation of large-scale organizations. The limitations of bureaucracy can thus be overcome by avoiding the use of bureaucracy.[20] This is not, however, a very realistic option today, since societies have no choice but to rely upon the talents of bureaucrats in areas like foreign affairs and national defense where some of their most pressing problems lie. On the domestic side the public demands a great and growing variety of services that inevitably require the attention of organized officialdom.

If the inevitability of a bureaucratized society is accepted, reliance must be placed instead upon the development of institutional mechanisms for mitigating some of the worst effects of decision-

[19] See pp. 104–108.

[20] For some suggestive comments on this alternative, see James Q. Wilson, "The Bureaucracy Problem," *The Public Interest*, No. 6 (Winter, 1967), pp. 3–9.

making through giant organizations. One device that is coming into increasing vogue is the *ombudsman* — an administrative official charged to help citizens obtain remedies for decisions by an executive agency that inflict unjustified injury upon them. This device, developed originally in Sweden, has spread to other countries as well, and is being increasingly urged as a solution to the problems of bureaucratization in all societies. One of the major factors underlying this resort to the *ombudsman* device is the expectation that such an official's activities will make policy more sensitive to the needs and interests of individuals whose circumstances may not fit neatly into the categories into which bureaucrats choose to divide the population.[21]

Increasingly, also, efforts are being made to find ways and means of building the viewpoints of the public into policy in the process of its initial development rather than as a result of feedback from enforcement problems. The most striking example of this we have had in recent history has been the attempt on the part of the Office of Economic Opportunity to provide for maximum feasible representation of the poor in local agencies responsible for carrying on OEO's war on poverty. The participation of the poor is required in both the agencies of local government which operate community action programs, and the private organizations which are authorized to participate in the administration of OEO's antipoverty activities.

The technique of allowing the members of affected groups to become involved in policy decisions is far from a new departure in American administration.[22] Farmers have long been granted the right to participate in deciding many questions in agricultural policy either by direct vote, or by representation in advisory groups that have a dominant role in policy decisions. Techniques of representing the public in the process of policy development are also prominent in the operation of the Selective Service System,

[21] The role of the *ombudsman* has attracted growing attention in the literature of public administration. See especially Walter Gellhorn, *Ombudsmen and Others: Citizens' Protectors in Nine Countries* (Cambridge: Harvard University Press, 1967) and Donald C. Rowat (ed.), *The Ombudsman: Citizen's Defender* (London: Allen & Unwin, 1965).

[22] For a careful examination of the use of this and other methods of controlling administrative behavior, see Charles E. Gilbert, "The Framework of Administrative Responsibility," *The Journal of Politics*, Vol. 21 (August, 1959), pp. 373–407.

grazing administration as carried on by the Bureau of Land Management in the West, and the activities of the Tennessee Valley Authority in the South.

In addition, a great number of agencies, including the Department of State, follow public opinion polls (or even conduct their own), systematically review editorials in newspapers, and letters to the editor columns, or in other ways try to keep abreast of changing currents of public opinion. Hopefully, the perception by government officials of these various manifestations of public response to what they are doing will allow them to "anticipate the reactions" of the public in designing official policy.[23]

However, an effective system of representing clientele in the development of policy differs substantially from arrangements under which executive officials themselves take public opinion into account in their policy decisions. In the case of a genuine system of representation, the public has an opportunity to speak for itself. When public opinion filters instead through the lens of bureaucratic perceptions, the image that emerges may be grossly distorted — reflecting not the actual contours of opinion but the image that it is convenient for bureaucrats to see.[24]

The future will thus present a continuing challenge to find techniques for controlling bureaucracy that will keep pace with the expansion of bureaucratic power. In the past, democratic societies have exhibited impressive powers of invention in this regard. However, a variety of circumstances in modern life, including especially the growing weight of expert knowledge in policy formation, continue to push bureaucracy toward a position of pre-eminence in the governing process. As we have seen, this bureaucratic power rests partly on the extraordinary capacities of public agencies as sources of expertise, and partly on the fact that administrative agencies have become major centers for the mobilization of political

23 For a discussion of the way in which the "anticipated reactions" of citizens may thus affect official behavior, see Friedrich, *op. cit.*, pp. 15–16.

24 *Cf.*, for example, the description of the "trustee" relationship between administrative officials and their public in Robert S. Friedman, Bernard W. Klein, and John H. Romani, "Administrative Agencies and the Publics They Serve," *Public Administration Review*, Vol. XXVI (September, 1966), p. 195: "a trustee . . . is satisfied with the knowledge that his constituents are supportive of his decisions and is likely to read the absence of complaints by constituents as support or acceptance."

energy and support. As a result, bureaucratic politics rather than party politics has become the dominant theater of decision in the modern state. The adjustment of democratic society to this fact continues to demand all the resourceful ingenuity of which it is capable.

Selected Bibliography

Alger, Chadwick F. "The External Bureaucracy in United States Foreign Affairs," *Administrative Science Quarterly*, Vol. 7 (June, 1962), 50–78.

Altshuler, Alan A. *The City Planning Process*. Ithaca, N.Y.: Cornell University Press, 1965.

Bachrach, Peter, and Morton S. Baratz. "Two Faces of Power," *American Political Science Review*, Vol. LVI (December, 1962), 947–952.

——————. "Decisions and Nondecisions: An Analytical Framework," *American Political Science Review*, Vol. LVII (September, 1963), 632–642.

Banfield, Edward C. *Political Influence*. New York: Free Press of Glencoe, 1961.

Bell, Daniel. "Comment: Government by Commission," *The Public Interest*, No. 3 (Spring, 1966), 3–9.

Bernstein, Marver H. *Regulating Business by Independent Commission*. Princeton, N.J.: Princeton University Press, 1955.

——————. *The Job of the Federal Executive*. Washington: The Brookings Institution, 1958.

Boyer, William W. "Policy Making by Government Agencies," *Midwest Journal of Political Science*, Vol. IV (August, 1960), 267–288.

Braybrooke, David. "The Mystery of Executive Success Re-examined," *Administrative Science Quarterly*, Vol. 8 (March, 1964), 533–560.

——————, and Charles E. Lindblom. *A Strategy of Decision*. New York: Free Press of Glencoe, 1963.

Brodie, Bernard. "The Scientific Strategists," in Robert Gilpin and Christopher Wright (eds.), *Scientists and National Policy-Making*. New York: Columbia University Press, 1964.

Brown, MacAlister. "The Demise of State Department Public Opinion Polls: A Study in Legislative Oversight," *Midwest Journal of Political Science*, Vol. V (February, 1961), 1–17.

Cater, Douglass. *The Fourth Branch of Government*. Boston: Houghton Mifflin Co., 1959.

Clark, Burton R. "Organizational Adaptation and Precarious Values: A Case Study," *American Sociological Review*, Vol. 21 (June, 1956), 327–336.

Cohen, Bernard. *The Press and Foreign Policy.* Princeton, N.J.: Princeton University Press, 1963.

Corson, John J. and R. Shale Paul. *Men Near the Top.* Baltimore: The Johns Hopkins Press, 1966.

Cotter, Cornelius P., and J. Malcolm Smith. "Administrative Responsibility: Congressional Prescription of Interagency Relationships," *Western Political Quarterly,* Vol. X (December, 1957), 765–782.

Crozier, Michel. *The Bureaucratic Phenomenon.* Chicago: University of Chicago Press, 1964.

Dahl, Robert A. *Who Governs?* New Haven: Yale University Press, 1961.

————, and Charles E. Lindblom. *Politics, Economics, and Welfare.* New York: Harper & Bros., 1953.

Dawson, Raymond H. "Congressional Innovation and Intervention in Defense Policy: Legislative Authorization of Weapons Systems," *American Political Science Review,* Vol. LVI (March, 1962), 42–57.

Dimock, Marshall E. "The Role of Discretion in Modern Administration," in John M. Gaus, Leonard D. White, and Marshall E. Dimock (eds.), *The Frontiers of Public Administration.* Chicago: University of Chicago Press, 1936.

Drew, Elizabeth B. "HEW Grapples with PPBS," *The Public Interest,* No. 8 (Summer, 1967), 9–29.

Dror, Yehezkel. "Muddling Through — 'Science' or Inertia?," *Public Administration Review,* Vol. XXIV (September, 1964), 153–157.

————. "Policy Analysts: A New Professional Role in Government Service," *Public Administration Review,* Vol. XXVII (September, 1967), 197–203.

Edelman, Murray. *The Symbolic Uses of Politics.* Urbana, Illinois: The University of Illinois Press, 1964.

Elder, Robert E. *The Policy Machine: The Department of State and American Foreign Policy.* Syracuse: Syracuse University Press, 1960.

Etzioni, Amitai. "Authority Structure and Organizational Effectiveness," *Administrative Science Quarterly,* Vol. 4 (June, 1959), 43–67.

————. *A Comparative Analysis of Complex Organizations.* New York: Free Press of Glencoe, 1961.

————. *Modern Organizations.* Englewood Cliffs, N.J.: Prentice-Hall, 1964.

————. "Mixed-Scanning: A 'Third' Approach to Decision-Making," *Public Administration Review,* Vol. XXVII (December, 1967), 385–392.

Evans, Allan. "Intelligence and Policy Formation," *World Politics,* Vol. XII (October, 1959), 84–91.

Fainsod, Merle. "Some Reflections on the Nature of the Regulatory Process," in Carl J. Friedrich and Edward S. Mason (eds.), *Public Policy*, Vol. I. Cambridge: Harvard University Press, 1940.

Falk, Stanley L. "The National Security Council Under Truman, Eisenhower, and Kennedy," *Political Science Quarterly*, Vol. LXXIX (September, 1964), 403–434.

Fenno, Richard F. *The Power of the Purse*. Boston: Little, Brown and Co., 1966.

————. *The President's Cabinet*. Cambridge: Harvard University Press, 1959.

Finer, Herman. "Administrative Responsibility in Democratic Government," *Public Administration Review*, Vol. I (Summer, 1941), 335–350.

Flash, Edward S., Jr. *Economic Advice and Presidential Leadership*. New York: Columbia University Press, 1965.

Foss, Phillip O. *Politics and Grass*. Seattle: University of Washington Press, 1960.

Freeman, J. Leiper. *The Political Process: Executive Bureau-Legislative Committee Relations*. New York: Random House, revised edition, 1965.

————. "The Bureaucracy in Pressure Politics," *Annals* of the American Academy of Political and Social Science, Vol. 319 (September, 1958), 10–19.

Friedman, Robert S., Bernard W. Klein, and John H. Romani. "Administrative Agencies and the Publics They Serve," *Public Administration Review*, Vol. XXVI (September, 1966), 192–204.

Friedrich, Carl J. "Public Policy and the Nature of Administrative Responsibility," in Carl J. Friedrich and Edward S. Mason (eds.), *Public Policy*, Vol. I. Cambridge: Harvard University Press, 1940.

Gerth, H. H. and C. Wright Mills. *From Max Weber: Essays in Sociology*. New York: Oxford University Press, 1946, 196–244.

Gilbert, Charles E. "The Framework of Administrative Responsibility," *Journal of Politics*, Vol. 21 (August, 1959), 373–407.

————. "Policy-Making in Public Welfare: The 1962 Amendments," *Political Science Quarterly*, Vol. LXXXI (June, 1966), 196–224.

Gilpin, Robert and Christopher Wright (eds.). *Scientists and National Policy-Making*. New York: Columbia University Press, 1964.

Green, Philip. "Science, Government and the Case of RAND: A Singular Pluralism," *World Politics*, Vol. XX (January, 1968), 301–326.

Greenberg, Daniel S. "The Myth of the Scientific Elite," *The Public Interest*, Vol. 1 (Fall, 1965), 51–62.

_____. *The Politics of Pure Science*. New York: New American Library, 1968.

Halperin, Morton H. "The Gaither Committee and the Policy Process," *World Politics,* Vol. XIII (April, 1961), 360–384.

Hammond, Paul Y. "The National Security Council as a Device for Interdepartmental Coordination," *American Political Science Review*, Vol. LIV (December, 1960), 899–910.

_____. "Foreign Policy-Making and Administrative Politics," *World Politics,* Vol. XVII (July, 1965), 656–671.

Hardin, Charles M. "The Bureau of Agricultural Economics Under Fire: A Study in Valuation Conflicts," *Journal of Farm Economics,* Vol. XXVIII (August, 1946), 635–668.

_____. *The Politics of Agriculture*. Glencoe, Ill.: The Free Press, 1952.

Harris, Joseph P. *Congressional Control of Administration*. N.Y.: Doubleday Anchor edition, 1965.

Hart, Henry C. *The Dark Missouri*. Madison: University of Wisconsin Press, 1957.

Haviland, H. Field, Jr. "Foreign Aid and the Policy Process: 1957," *American Political Science Review,* Vol. LII (September, 1958), 689–724.

Hearle, Edward F. R. "How Useful Are 'Scientific' Tools of Management?," *Public Administration Review,* Vol. XXI (Autumn, 1961), 206–209.

Hebal, John J. "Generalist Versus Specialist in the Bureau of Indian Affairs," *Public Administration Review,* Vol. XXI (Winter, 1961), 16–22.

Held, Virginia. "PPBS Comes to Washington," *The Public Interest,* No. 4 (Summer, 1966), 102–115.

Herring, E. Pendleton. *Public Administration and the Public Interest*. New York: McGraw-Hill, 1936.

Heyman, Victor K. "Government by Contract: Boon or Boner?," *Public Administration Review,* Vol. XXI (Spring, 1961), 59–64.

Hilsman, Roger. "Congressional-Executive Relations and the Foreign Policy Consensus," *American Political Science Review,* Vol. LII (September, 1958), 725–744.

Hitch, Charles J. *Decision-Making for Defense*. Berkeley and Los Angeles: University of California Press, 1965.

Holden, Matthew, Jr. " 'Imperialism' in Bureaucracy," *American Political Science Review,* Vol. LX (December, 1966), 943–951.

Huntington, Samuel P. "The Marasmus of the I.C.C.: The Commission, the Railroads, and the Public Interest," *Yale Law Journal,* Vol. 61 (April, 1952), 467–509.

————. *The Soldier and the State.* Cambridge: Harvard University Press, 1957.

————. *The Common Defense: Strategic Programs in National Politics.* New York: Columbia University Press, 1961.

Hyneman, Charles S. *Bureaucracy in a Democracy.* New York: Harper & Bros., 1950.

Jacob, Charles E. *Policy and Bureaucracy.* New York: D. Van Nostrand, 1966.

Jacob, Herbert, and Kenneth N. Vines (eds.). *Politics in the American States.* Boston: Little, Brown and Co., 1965.

Janowitz, Morris. *The Professional Soldier.* New York: Free Press of Glencoe, 1960.

Jennings, M. Kent. *Community Influentials.* New York: Free Press of Glencoe, 1964.

————, Milton C. Cummings, Jr., and Franklin P. Kilpatrick. "Trusted Leaders: Perceptions of Appointed Federal Officials," *Public Opinion Quarterly,* Vol. 30 (Fall, 1966), 368–384.

Kaufman, Herbert. "Emerging Conflicts in the Doctrines of Public Administration," *American Political Science Review,* Vol. L (December, 1956), 1057–1073.

————. *The Forest Ranger.* Baltimore: The Johns Hopkins Press, 1960.

Keiser, Norman F. "Public Responsibility and Federal Advisory Groups: A Case Study," *Western Political Quarterly,* Vol. XI (June, 1958), 251–264.

Kerr, James R. "Congress and Space: Overview or Oversight?," *Public Administration Review,* Vol. XXV (September, 1965), 185–192.

Knorr, Klaus. "Failures in National Intelligence Estimates: The Case of the Cuban Missiles," *World Politics,* Vol. XVI (April, 1964), 455–467.

————. "On the Cost-Effectiveness Approach to Military Research and Development," *Bulletin of the Atomic Scientists,* Vol. XXII (November, 1966), 11–14.

Kroll, Morton. "Hypotheses and Designs for the Study of Public Policies in the United States," *Midwest Journal of Political Science,* Vol. VI (November, 1962), 363–383.

La Palombara, Joseph (ed.). *Bureaucracy and Political Development.* Princeton: Princeton University Press, 1963.

Leiserson, Avery. "Political Limitations on Executive Reorganization," *American Political Science Review,* Vol. XLI (February, 1947), 68–84.

————. "Scientists and the Policy Process," *American Political Science Review,* Vol. LIX (June, 1965), 408–416.

Lindblom, Charles E. "Policy Analysis," *American Economic Review*, Vol. 48 (June, 1958), 298–312.

_____. *The Intelligence of Democracy*. New York: Free Press of Glencoe, 1965.

Long, Norton. *The Polity*. Chicago: Rand McNally & Co., 1962.

Lowi, Theodore J. "American Business, Public Policy, Case Studies, and Political Theory," *World Politics*, Vol. XVI (July, 1964), 677–715.

Maass, Arthur. *Muddy Waters*. Cambridge: Harvard University Press, 1951.

_____. "Benefit-Cost Analysis: Its Relevance to Public Investment Decisions," *Quarterly Journal of Economics*, Vol. LXXX (May, 1966), 208–226.

Macmahon, Arthur W. "Congressional Oversight of Administration: The Power of the Purse," *Political Science Quarterly*, Vol. LVIII (June, 1943), 161–190; (September, 1943), 380–414.

Mann, Dean E. "The Selection of Federal Political Executives," *American Political Science Review*, Vol. LVIII (March, 1964), 81–99.

Mann, Seymour Z. "Policy Formulation in the Executive Branch: The Taft-Hartley Experience," *Western Political Quarterly*, Vol. XIII (September, 1960), 597–608.

March, James G. and Herbert A. Simon. *Organizations*. New York: John Wiley & Sons, 1958.

Martin, Laurence W. "The Market for Strategic Ideas in Britain: The 'Sandys Era,'" *American Political Science Review*, Vol. LVI (March, 1962), 23–41.

Marx, Fritz Morstein (ed.). *Elements of Public Administration*. Englewood Cliffs, N.J.: Prentice-Hall, 2nd edition, 1959.

Moos, Malcolm, and Francis E. Rourke. *The Campus and the State*. Baltimore: The Johns Hopkins Press, 1959.

Morgan, Robert J. "Pressure Politics and Resources Administration," *Journal of Politics*, Vol. 18 (February, 1956), 39–60.

Neustadt, Richard E. "Presidency and Legislation: The Growth of Central Clearance," *American Political Science Review*, Vol. XLVIII (September, 1954), 641–671.

_____. "Presidency and Legislation: Planning the President's Program," *American Political Science Review*, Vol. XLIX (December, 1955), 980–1021.

_____. *Presidential Power*. New York: John Wiley & Sons, 1960.

_____. "Approaches to Staffing the Presidency: Notes on FDR and

JFK," *American Political Science Review,* Vol. LVII (December, 1963), 855–864.

Nieburg, H. L. "The Eisenhower AEC and Congress: A Study in Executive-Legislative Relations," *Midwest Journal of Political Science,* Vol. VI (May, 1962), 115–148.

Orlans, Harold. *Contracting for Atoms.* Washington: The Brookings Institution, 1967.

Peabody, Robert L., and Francis E. Rourke. "Public Bureaucracies," in James G. March (ed.), *Handbook of Organizations.* Chicago: Rand McNally & Co., 1965.

Penniman, Clara. "Reorganization and the Internal Revenue Service," *Public Administration Review,* Vol. 21 (Summer, 1961), 121–130.

Pipe, G. Russell. "Congressional Liaison: The Executive Branch Consolidates Its Relations with Congress," *Public Administration Review,* Vol. XXVI (March, 1966), 14–24.

Posvar, Wesley W. "The Impact of Strategy Expertise on the National Security Policy of the U.S.," in John D. Montgomery and Arthur Smithies (eds.), *Public Policy,* Vol. XIII. Cambridge: Harvard University Press, 1964.

Price, Don K. *Government and Science.* New York: New York University Press, 1954.

————. *The Scientific Estate.* Cambridge: Harvard University Press, 1965.

Public Administration Review. "Planning-Programming Budgeting System: A Symposium," Vol. 26 (December, 1966), 243–310.

Ransom, Harry Howe. *Can American Democracy Survive Cold War?* Garden City, N.Y.: Doubleday Anchor Books, 1964.

Reagan, Michael D. "The Political Structure of the Federal Reserve System," *American Political Science Review,* Vol. LV (March, 1961), 64–76.

Redford, Emmette S. *Administration of National Economic Control.* New York: The Macmillan Co., 1952.

Rhode, W. E. *Committee Clearance of Administrative Decisions.* East Lansing: Michigan State University Press, 1959.

Riggs, Fred W. "Bureaucracy and Political Development: A Paradoxical View," in Joseph La Palombara (ed.), *Bureaucracy and Political Development.* Princeton: Princeton University Press, 1963.

Ripley, Randall B. "Interagency Committees and Incrementalism: The Case of Aid to India," *Midwest Journal of Political Science,* Vol. VIII (May, 1964), 143–165.

Rourke, Francis E. "The Department of Labor and the Trade Unions," *Western Political Quarterly,* Vol. VII (December, 1954), 656–672.

————. "The Politics of Administrative Organization: A Case History," *Journal of Politics,* Vol. 19 (August, 1957), 461–478.

————. *Secrecy and Publicity: Dilemmas of Democracy.* Baltimore: The Johns Hopkins Press, 1961.

————, and Glenn E. Brooks. *The Managerial Revolution in Higher Education.* Baltimore: The Johns Hopkins Press, 1966.

Saletan, Elma M. "Administrative Trustification," *Western Political Quarterly,* Vol. XI (December, 1958), 857–874.

Sayre, Wallace (ed.). *The Federal Government Service.* Englewood Cliffs, N.J.: Prentice-Hall, 1965.

————, and Herbert Kaufman. *Governing New York City.* New York: Russell Sage Foundation, 1960.

Schaller, Lyle E. "Is the Citizen Advisory Committee a Threat to Representative Government?," *Public Administration Review,* Vol. XXIV (September, 1964), 175–179.

Scher, Seymour. "Congressional Committee Members as Independent Agency Overseers: A Case Study," *American Political Science Review,* Vol. LIV (December, 1960), 911–920.

————. "Regulatory Agency Control Through Appointment: The Case of the Eisenhower Administration and the NLRB," *Journal of Politics,* Vol. 23 (November, 1961), 667–688.

Schick, Allen. "The Road to PPB: The Stages of Budget Reform," *Public Administration Review,* Vol. XXVI (December, 1966), 243–258.

Schiff, Ashley L. *Fire and Water: Scientific Heresy in the Forest Service.* Cambridge: Harvard University Press, 1962.

————. "Innovation and Administrative Decision-Making: A Study of the Conservation of Land Resources," *Administrative Science Quarterly,* Vol. 11 (June, 1966), 1–30.

Schilling, Warner R. "The H-Bomb Decision: How to Decide Without Actually Choosing." *Political Science Quarterly,* Vol. LXXVI (March, 1961), 24–46.

————. "Scientists, Foreign Policy, and Politics," in Robert Gilpin and Christopher Wright (eds.), *Scientists and National Policy-Making.* New York: Columbia University Press, 1964.

Schlesinger, Arthur M., Jr. *The Coming of the New Deal.* Boston: Houghton Mifflin Co., 1959.

Schubert, Glendon. *The Public Interest.* New York: Free Press of Glencoe, 1960.

Selznick, Philip. *TVA and the Grass Roots*. Berkeley: University of California Press, 1949.

————, *Leadership in Administration*. Evanston, Illinois: Row, Peterson, & Co. 1957.

Senate Subcommittee on National Security and International Operations, *Planning-Programming-Budgeting*, 90th Cong., 1st session, committee print, August 11, 1967. The hearings and reports of this subcommittee provide a wealth of information on the policy process in the area of national security affairs.

Shapiro, Martin. *The Supreme Court and Administrative Agencies*. New York: Free Press. 1968.

Sharkansky, Ira. "Four Agencies and an Appropriations Subcommittee: A Comparative Study of Budget Strategies," *Midwest Journal of Political Science*, Vol. IX (August, 1965), 254–281.

————. "An Appropriations Subcommittee and Its Client Agencies: A Comparative Study of Supervision and Control," *American Political Science Review*, Vol. LIX (September, 1965), 622–628.

Shils, Edward A. "The Legislator and His Environment," *University of Chicago Law Review*, Vol. 18 (Spring, 1951), 571–584.

Shultz, George P., and Thomas L. Whisler (eds.). *Management Organization and the Computer*. New York: Free Press of Glencoe, 1960.

Simon, Herbert A. *Administrative Behavior*. New York: The Macmillan Co., 2nd edition, 1957.

————. *The New Science of Management Decision*. New York: Harper & Row, 1960.

————, Donald W. Smithburg, and Victor Thompson. *Public Administration*. New York: Alfred A. Knopf, 1950.

Smith, Bruce L. R. *The Rand Corporation: Case Study of a Nonprofit Advisory Corporation*. Cambridge: Harvard University Press, 1966.

Smith, J. Malcolm, and Cornelius P. Cotter. "Administrative Accountability: Reporting to Congress," *Western Political Quarterly*, Vol. X (June, 1957), 405–415.

Somers, Herman M. *Presidential Agency*. Cambridge: Harvard University Press, 1950.

Sorauf, Frank J. "The Public Interest Reconsidered," *Journal of Politics*, Vol. 19 (November, 1957), 616–639.

Sorensen, Theodore C. *Decision-Making in the White House*. New York: Columbia University Press, 1963.

Stein, Harold (ed.). *Public Administration and Policy Development*. New York: Harcourt, Brace, 1952. A collection of case studies on public administration and policy formation published under the auspices of the Inter-University Case program. For a bibliography of all the ICP case studies published through 1967, see W. Henry Lambright, *Shooting Down the Nuclear Plane*, Indianapolis: Bobbs-Merrill Co., Inc., 1967.

Steiner, Gilbert Y. *Social Insecurity: The Politics of Welfare*. Chicago: Rand McNally & Co., 1966.

Tanenhaus, Joseph. "Supreme Court Attitudes Toward Federal Administrative Agencies," *Journal of Politics*, Vol. 22 (August, 1960), 502–524.

Thompson, James D., and William J. McEwen. "Organizational Goals and Environment: Goal-Setting As An Interaction Process," *American Sociological Review*, Vol. 23 (February, 1958), 23–31.

Thompson, Victor A. *The Regulatory Process in OPA Rationing*. New York: Columbia University Press, 1950.

————. *Modern Organization*. New York: Alfred A. Knopf, 1961.

Tomasek, Robert D. "The Migrant Problem and Pressure Group Politics," *Journal of Politics*, Vol. 23 (May, 1961), 295–319.

Truman, David B. *The Governmental Process*. New York: Alfred A. Knopf, 1951.

Waldo, Dwight. *The Administrative State*. New York: The Ronald Press. 1948.

Wengert, Norman. *Natural Resources and the Political Struggle*. Garden City, N.Y.: Doubleday & Co., 1955.

Wildavsky, Aaron. *Dixon-Yates: A Study in Power Politics*. New Haven: Yale University Press, 1962.

————. "The Analysis of Issue-Contexts in the Study of Decision-Making," *Journal of Politics*, Vol. 24 (November, 1962), 717–732.

————. *The Politics of the Budgetary Process*. Boston: Little, Brown and Co., 1964.

————, and Arthur Hammond. "Comprehensive versus Incremental Budgeting in the Department of Agriculture," *Administrative Science Quarterly*, Vol. 10 (December, 1965), 321–346.

Wilensky, Harold L. *Organizational Intelligence*. New York: Basic Books, Inc., 1967.

Wilson, James Q. "Innovation in Organization: Notes Toward a Theory," in James D. Thompson (ed.), *Approaches to Organizational Design*. Pittsburgh: University of Pittsburgh Press, 1966.

————. "The Bureaucracy Problem," *The Public Interest*, No. 6 (Winter, 1967), 3–9.

Witte, Edwin E. "The Preparation of Proposed Legislative Measures by Administrative Departments," in U.S. President's Committee on Administrative Management, *Report with Special Studies.* Washington, D.C.: U.S. Government Printing Office, 1937.

Yarmolinsky, Adam. "Ideas Into Programs," *The Public Interest,* No. 2 (Winter, 1966), 70–79.

Zeigler, Harmon. *Interest Groups in American Society.* Englewood Cliffs, N.J.: Prentice-Hall, 1964.

Index

167

DATE DUE
